A Lay Guide to ROMANS

J. C. Wenger

Foreword by Walter A. Elwell

HERALD PRESS
Scottdale, Pennsylvania
Kitchener, Ontario
1983

Library of Congress Cataloging in Publication Data

Wenger, J. C. (John Christian), 1910-
  A lay guide to Romans.

  1. Bible. N. T. Romans—Commentaries. I. Bible.
N. T. Romans. II. Title.
BS2665.3.W4 1983   227'.107   82-15789
ISBN 0-8361-3316-1 (pbk.)

Unless otherwise noted, Bible quotations are from *The New International Version*, Copyright © 1978 by The New York International Bible Society. Used by permission of Zondervan Publishing House.

A LAY GUIDE TO ROMANS
Copyright © 1983 by Herald Press, Scottdale, Pa. 15683
    Published simultaneously in Canada by Herald Press,
    Kitchener, Ont. N2G 4M5
Library of Congress Catalog Card Number: 82-15789
International Standard Book Number: 0-8361-3316-1
Printed in the United States of America
Design by Alice B. Shetler

83 84 85 86 87 88 10 9 8 7 6 5 4 3 2 1

Contents

Foreword

In this commentary on Romans by J. C. Wenger the essence of Paul's thought has been thoroughly grasped. Wenger has assimilated and explained Romans in terms that can be readily understood. So often, when a Bible professor tackles the book of Romans the result is a complex *magnum opus* that is directed mainly to other scholars. While written in such a way that scholars will not be put off by it, *A Lay Guide to Romans* is not intended for them. Rather, this commentary is written for lay people who lack formal theological training, but are ready to think seriously about their faith. They will find a wealth of material here that can be put to use immediately in their lives.

Throughout the history of the church the book of Romans has played an important part. Being tied to the city of Rome by its name naturally led to its wide use as the Roman church gained ascendency. But it was more than that. The intrinsic merit of the book and its complex, well-thought out theology have appealed to scholar and lay person alike.

In the early days of the church, Augustine found his way out of a spiritual quandry by studying the book of Romans. Luther's well-known struggle in seeking righteousness by his own efforts was resolved by reading in Romans that we are justified by faith. John Wesley's "strange warmth" arose in connection with insights gained from the book of Romans. In our own day, the great theologian Karl Barth was drawn away from an old-line liberalism, in part, by reading Romans. His commentary on Romans marked the end of one era of theology and introduced another.

Clearly, the book of Romans has been pivotal at crucial moments in the life of God's people. What is its great appeal? No small part of its effectiveness is that Paul himself lived in a time of crisis in the history of the church. Romans reflects Paul's resolution of conflict within himself. It rings true to his experience, and also to ours. Paul was no ivory tower dreamer who surveyed the stresses of life aloofly from a distance. Rather he was involved in the difficult task of formulating and spreading the gospel to the Greco-Roman world. In the book of Romans his thought had matured enough so that a relatively precise statement could be made, but the reality of life is still felt.

The book contains well-formulated doctrine. Of all the letters Paul wrote, Romans is the most thorough and systematic in exploring the great ideas that sustain the church: God, man, sin, revelation, Christ, redemption, faith, reconciliation, the Holy Spirit, baptism—just to name a few. Another important dimension of the book is the spiritual insight it contains, again springing from crisis. Paul struggles with spiritual defeat in chapter 7, but rises to spiritual heights in chapter 8 when claiming for himself the certainties of the Christian faith. "What can separate us from the love of Christ?" he asks, and the answer is one we take for granted. "Nothing." Largely because of Paul we too may speak with such confidence.

Struggling with the soul-destroying pressures of his day, Paul learned through experience that if God be for us, nothing can be against us. Indeed, he discovered in his own life that God can work *all* things together for good to those who love the Lord and are called according to his purpose. The measure of Paul's maturity, and ours, is the ability to live according to that realization. If we could only see beyond the surface of what takes place to the larger reality of God and his will, we would be able to live lives free from anxiety, as Jesus promised. We must dare to believe that no ultimate harm can come to those who are God's, no matter how difficult our circumstances might be.

A refreshing emphasis runs throughout *A Lay Guide to Romans*. Although deeply committed to his Mennonite tradition, the author appreciates the good in other traditions as well. He quotes from a variety of sources, as long as the essential truth is served. This makes the commentary useful to Christians in general, not just to members of certain denominations. The basic truths are held with tenacity, but charity rules over all.

Reading *A Lay Guide to Romans* by J. C. Wenger will deepen a person's Christian life, challenge one's theological understanding, and increase one's biblical knowledge—in short, it will make better Christians of us all.

Walter A. Elwell
Christianity Today

Preface

In this commentary I have attempted to give the meaning of the *Romans* text in crisp and clear English. It will be evident to the reader that I hold to the accuracy and reliability of the *New International Version* of the Bible (1978); indeed, it was my joy to serve from the beginning of the project (1965) on what was first known as the "Committee of Fifteen," later as the "Committee on Bible Translation." But I wrote this commentary on the Greek text of Romans, employing the text of the United Bible Societies. To the best of my ability I have sought to give the meaning of Paul's original words and sentences.

The literature on Romans is overwhelming. Note, for example, the 190 commentaries cited in *Meyer's Commentary* (German, 1872; English, 1884). Among the better works on Romans now available may be listed those by Barth, Calvin, Cranfield, Erdman, Garvie, Godet, Harrison, Käsemann, Lange, Lenski, Luther, Meyer, Minear, Moule, Murray, Newell, Nygren, Parry, Sanday and Headlam, and Stendahl. Naturally I also made much use of standard works on Greek grammar, text, and lexicography.

It will be obvious to the reader that I am fond of the writings of the sixteenth-century Frisian reformer, Menno Simons, who united with the peace wing of the Dutch Free Church led by Jacob van Campen (martyred 1535) and by Obbe and Dirk Philips. Menno made many incisive comments on Romans which I have taken the liberty to quote in an appendix at the end. Each chapter includes appropriate comments by Menno. In this connection, the "Index to Scripture Quotations and Allusions" in Menno's *Complete Writings,* made by Ira D. Landis, was helpful.

My Associated Mennonite Biblical Seminaries colleagues, Dean Jacob W. Elias and Willard M. Swartley, and my fellow ministers, Levi C. Hartzler and Clare Schumm, read the manuscript carefully and shared generously numerous suggestions for the improvement of the manuscript. For this help I wish to thank them warmly.

It has been an enriching and heartwarming experience to work through once more what I regard as Paul's *magnum opus.* I hope the reader will catch something of the enthusiasm which I have again felt for this great epistle. *Soli Deo Gloria!*

J. C. Wenger
Goshen, Indiana

A
Lay Guide to
ROMANS

Introduction

Meet the Author

The author probably had a Jewish name from the beginning (Saul), as well as a Gentile name for use in the non-Jewish world (Paul). In the book of Acts he is called Saul all through his life in the Jewish world, and only on the first missionary journey is he introduced to the reader as having a second name, Paul.

Paul's Background

Scholars believe that Paul was born in the first decade of the first century. His parents were strict Pharisees who spoke Aramaic (called Hebrew in the first-century world, but a sister language to the Hebrew of Moses and the prophets). Paul's birthplace was Tarsus, the capital of the province of Cilicia in Asia Minor (now Turkey) and the seat of one of the three great academies of that day (Athens, Alexandria, Tarsus). Paul's father somehow became a Roman citizen. This was a privilege passed on to his gifted son which stood Paul in good stead many times during his long and effective service for Christ. Paul belonged to the tribe of Benjamin; as a typical Jewish boy, he learned a trade—tentmaking in his case, one who made "small portable tents of cloth of goats' hair or linen" (Thayer). Some commentators think that his chief task was to weave the material of which tents were made.

Before Conversion

In his early youth Paul's devout parents sent him to Jerusalem to study under the able and renowned Gamaliel, a grandson of the even more famous Hillel. Both Paul's father and Gamaliel were Pharisees, and Paul became an intense and devout member of that group. As such he hated the group called "The Way," that body of believers who accepted Jesus as the Messiah (Christ in Greek) of Old Testament prophecy. Paul regarded Jesus as a phony messiah, and he became a fierce persecutor of the Christians, arresting men and women, and having them scourged and jailed. He participated even in the group which stoned the Christian martyr Stephen to death.

Christ Arrests Paul

Paul was likely trilingual, knowing the Hebrew of the Old Testament, Aramaic as his mother tongue, and Greek, the language of the Greco-Roman world of his day. He may have known Latin, also. A man of immense intellect, of an iron will, and yet of a warm heart, he labored hard to eliminate the new "heresy" from the earth. Securing written authorization from the Jewish high priest, he set out about the year AD 35 for the city of Damascus intending to arrest any Christians he found there and bring them in chains to Jerusalem for trial and imprisonment. As he and his party approached Damascus, a brilliant light, brighter than the sun, shone upon him and the risen and enthroned Lord Jesus addressed him in his mother tongue Aramaic, calling out to him, "Saul, Saul." To get the full story one must read all three accounts (Acts 9, 22, and 26). A blind and broken Saul was led into Damascus. On the third day the Lord Jesus appeared to a disciple named Ananias and commissioned him to baptize and lay hands on the new convert, whereupon he regained his sight and was filled with the Holy Spirit. Immediately he preached Christ in the synagogues of Damascus.

Retreat to Arabia

Without any clear explanation, the New Testament reports that Paul then spent three years (which could have meant one full year and parts of two others) in Arabia. It is supposed that during this time Paul was in a quiet retreat to meditate, pray, and read the Old Testament with Holy Spirit illumination—which enabled the erstwhile persecutor to see it in a new light. For the prophets had written much of the sufferings and subsequent glories of the Messiah, which the Christians believed were about Jesus of Nazareth.

Tarsus to Antioch

During the remainder of his life Paul made only brief visits to Jerusalem; he mentions, for example, a fifteen-day visit with Peter. For a number of years he lived in his hometown of Tarsus. But the Spirit of Christ was about to catapult Paul into the very center of his Great Commission—to send him all over the civilized world of southern Europe to establish a chain of congregations from Jerusalem to Rome, and perhaps all the way to Spain. It all came about in a strange manner.

Within a decade of the crucifixion and resurrection of Christ, a vigorous congregation of believers developed in the large city of Antioch in Syria, a metropolis of half a million people. Both Jews and Gentiles were members, and the Jewish leaders of the Jerusalem Church dispatched one of their finest members, a man named Barnabas, to go down to Antioch to examine the situation. Spirit-filled as he was, Barnabas reacted with holy joy to what he found at Antioch, and it occurred to him that he knew just the man to help lead the new believers to greater maturity in Christ. So off he went to Tarsus and brought Paul back with him. Then the Antioch church enjoyed rich Bible study for a whole year under the leadership of Barnabas and Paul.

First Missionary Journey

No one anticipated the next step—no one but God.

Probably through a prophet the Lord called for the commissioning of Barnabas and Paul to carry the good news of salvation through Christ out into the Roman world. Consequently, in a solemn ceremony of prayer and the laying-on of hands, these two men of God were sent forth. This first missionary journey probably took place in the late forties of the first century. And great was the rejoicing of the church when Barnabas and Paul later reported how God had blessed their ministry of the Word.

Apostolic Conference at Jerusalem

Unfortunately there was a radical Jewish party in the church at Jerusalem who simply could not believe that the ceremonial law of Moses had been discontinued with the coming of Christ. Coming to Antioch they caused no little confusion in the church with their Judaizing notions. It was finally decided to send a delegation to the apostles and elders at Jerusalem about this issue. Paul and Barnabas were naturally a part of the group. The story of this apostolic conference of about AD 50 is told in Acts 15.

The consensus to which the Holy Spirit led was a ringing declaration of "Christian freedom" coupled with a few gracious concessions to the Jewish conscience: not to eat foods offered to idols; not to eat blood (including the meat of strangled animals); and a special warning against the immorality of the Gentile world. This report caused great joy in the congregations of the Greco-Roman world.

Second Missionary Journey

In the early fifties Paul and Silas set out on the second great missionary journey which took them across Asia Minor to Corinth and Athens. It was on this trip that Paul wrote his two little letters, 1 and 2 Thessalonians, the first two letters of a total of thirteen in the New Testament canon.

Third Missionary Journey

Paul's third missionary journey took place in the mid-fifties, around 54-58, during which time he spent over two years in Ephesus where he enjoyed a rich ministry of teaching and instructing not only the converts he had won, but also the entire church. Paul spent the last few months of this third journey at Corinth, probably in the spring of AD 58. Prior to these last few months Paul had written three great letters: Galatians and 1 and 2 Corinthians. Then at Corinth he wrote Romans, in some ways his greatest book, certainly the most thorough of his treatises on the divine plan of salvation.

Phoebe Leaving for Rome

We read from time to time of Paul's keen interest in the church at Rome and of his intense longing to visit them and fellowship with them in Christ. A woman named Phoebe of Cenchreae, the seaport of Corinth—apparently a member of the diaconate at Cenchreae—was about to set out on a journey to Rome. Paul dictated the Roman letter to a scribe named Tertius while a guest in the home of one of his Corinthian converts named Gaius. But it is only in the last section of Romans that Paul gets around to commending Phoebe to the "family" of Christians at Rome; then he attests to the fact that she had been a great help to many believers, including Paul himself, and asks the Roman church to "receive her in the Lord in a way worthy of the saints."

Paul Appeals His Case

The story of the remainder of Paul's life can be told quickly. He went up to Jerusalem, where Jewish hostility soon led to his arrest and imprisonment and even to a plan to assassinate him. Learning of the plot through a boy, the nephew of Paul, the Roman authorities hastily spirited him under heavy guard out of the city by night, and imprisoned him in Caesarea for two years (about AD 58-60). After seeing that he was a political pawn, and that he would likely never have a fair trial there, Paul made use of one of his rights as a Roman citizen: he appealed to the emperor. The winter of 60-61 Paul spent on his famous shipwreck journey to the capital city of the empire. *Acts* closes with the terse comment that Paul remained under house arrest in Rome for two years (about 61-63).

Paul's Later Years

The years in Rome were rich in many ways. Paul had opportunity to share the good news of salvation through Christ to the whole Praetorian Guard. He also wrote his four prison epistles: Colossians, Philemon, Ephesians, and Philippians. When Paul wrote these letters, he anticipated being released. The release evidently took place, for the circumstances described in the pastoral letters attributed to him (1 Timothy, Titus, and 2 Timothy) seem to reflect quite different circumstances—and a far different outlook. Paul then looked forward to his speedy end. Some scholars, especially those who maintain that Paul wrote the three pastoral letters, therefore assume that he was released from his Roman imprisonment, that he had a period of freedom (during which time he may have gone to Spain as he had long planned to do, for Clement of Rome wrote about AD 95 that Paul had indeed reached the "bounds of the West," i.e., Gibraltar), that he was again arrested, and finally executed about AD 67 by beheading.

Paul's Theological Stance

What a contribution this Jewish apostle to the Gentiles made to the church of his first-century generation—and to the church of all ages through his mighty letters! For Paul was second to none in the clarity with which he set forth the riches of being "in Christ" and in his masterful grasp of Jesus as the Messiah of Old Testament prophecy (cf. 2 Peter 3:15, 16). Paul was foremost a champion of Christian freedom—that no legalism characterizes the Christian life, but that the Holy Spirit so transforms Christian converts, and so fills them with holy love, that from the bottom of their hearts they long to be like Jesus and thus to please God.

The Church at Rome

Paul Taken to Rome

For a long time, as we saw, Paul had had a longing to visit the believers at Rome. He had hoped that he might be a blessing to the Christians at Rome; he knew that he himself would receive a blessing through fellowship with them. But little did Paul anticipate the way he would get to Rome—as a prisoner of the state! At the end of his third missionary journey he was arrested in Jerusalem and imprisoned first in Caesarea and then later in Rome after he had appealed for a hearing before the emperor. So he went to Rome as anything but a free man. Many of his friends had located in Rome; earlier Aquila and Priscilla had gone from Rome to Corinth because the Emperor Claudius had expelled the Jews from Rome in AD 52.

Origin of the Church in Rome

No record has been preserved of the founding of the church in Rome. We do know that visitors from Rome were present at Jerusalem on the Day of Pentecost when the enthroned Lord poured out the Holy Spirit in fullness on the waiting believers. At least some of those Roman visitors must have returned to the capital city as radiant believers and witnesses to the good news of salvation through Christ.

Jews and Gentiles United in the Church

There was also great ease of movement and travel in the Roman Empire of Paul's day. Because merchants, tradesmen, and people from all walks of life found it easy to move to Rome, a sizable number of Christians were surely found there at a very early date. Some were former Jews, and some were Gentiles; Paul was obviously aware of both groups as he wrote his great epistle to the Roman church. It was the most natural thing in the world for the Christians in Rome to find each other, and in Christ to want to worship God together. Therefore they began to meet regularly to sing the praises of their Lord, to listen to the reading of the Law and the Prophets, and to be taught the gospel by anointed messengers of God's truth who had come there as ministers, or who were chosen to serve as ministers by the young church in Rome.

A Glimpse at the Letter

The Basic Problem

In many respects Romans is the fullest and clearest exposition of Paul's theology of salvation. It is a model of literary clarity and organization. Its basic question is, "How can a person who is a sinner by nature become righteous in the sight of a holy God?"

Key Verses

Paul begins this epistle with a brief prologue which contains a greeting to the church in Rome. After a fleeting reference to the twofold nature of Christ, Paul goes on to express his interest in and love for the Roman church. He concludes his prologue with these key verses: "I am not ashamed of the gospel, because it is the power of God for the salvation of everyone who believes: first for the Jew, then for the Gentile. For in the gospel a righteousness from God is revealed, a righteousness that is by faith from first to last, just as it is written: [Habakkuk 2:4] 'The righteous will live by faith' " (1:16, 17).

Universal Sinfulness   1:16-17

Paul then switches suddenly to the severity of the sin problem in the human race. He first describes the Gentiles' perversity which initiated idolatry of the crudest type, perverting God's good gift of sexuality and abounding in all manner of sins. He then sternly warned of God's coming judgment on sin. Throughout this section of the letter the Jewish fathers could probably have stroked their beards with Pharisaic self-righteousness—how far they were from the idolatry and gross immorality of the heathen world! But Paul then turns on the Jews and shows them that they are really worse than the Gentiles, for guilt is commensurate with light; since they were entrusted with the "oracles" of God (the Old Testament Scriptures), they were under a divine obligation to live in holiness, love, and glad obedience. But they did not so live. Finally, in one citation after another from the Scriptures, Paul sets forth the dreadful truth that all human beings are sinners in thought, word, and deed. Therefore no amount of Law can save sinners, for people need more than a code to live by; they need a Savior to deliver them from the inclination to defy God and to live in sin.

God's Gift: Righteousness 3:21-31

This brings Paul to the richest section of the letter on the theme of the only righteousness which can save the sinner. Righteousness is not at all a personal achievement, Paul maintains. It is a gift from God to those who respond to the wooing and convicting power of the Holy Spirit. It is the righteousness which the Scriptures point to, that which God *gives* to his covenant believers. Only God can declare a person to be righteous. Only God can, in his amazing love and grace, fully accept a believing convert to Christ and give the convert a perfect standing before him. The Reformers took a Latin word and called this condition "justification by faith" It could just as well be called "righteousness by faith" or "gift righteousness." It is not the result of human obedience to the law of God. It is not the reward for living a perfect life or having a flawless character. It is the good news ("gospel") that God in sheer grace fully accepts everyone who turns from sin to Christ; he gives the gift of unearned and undeserved righteousness to each person willing to surrender to the Son of God. To make this truth live, Paul takes Abraham as a model of righteousness by faith.

Abraham as a Model 4

Actually Paul has three foundational passages from Holy Scripture on which he bases his teaching. In 1:17 he quoted Habakkuk 2:4 from the Greek version of the Old Testament, the

Septuagint. In Romans 4:3 he appeals to Genesis 15:6 that God credited Abraham's faith to him as righteousness. And in Romans 4:7, 8 Paul quotes Psalm 32:1, 2 on the blessings of being forgiven, of having a perfect standing before God. But more than that, Paul anticipates the argument of his Jewish friends that Abraham was, after all, man of good works (4:2). Wrong! cries Paul. Look again! It was not a matter of good works at all, but of the fact that Abraham believed God. It was the righteousness of faith which he received, not that of achievement. But, says the Jew, you are forgetting that Abraham had received the sacred sign of the old covenant, the holy rite of circumcision. Wrong again! says Paul. Abraham was first declared righteous on the basis of his faith. Only later did he receive the sign or seal of that righteousness which he already had before he received the sign. Finally, Abraham was not declared righteous on the basis of law, for all that law can do is show that we humans are sinners. Whereas the perfect righteousness and the perfect standing which Abraham enjoyed were through his faith. Paul goes on to describe the inner struggles which believing Abraham had, but he was in the end an example of trust, for he took a firm stand on the full trustworthiness of the promise of God. Abraham is a model for us to follow, for God will also declare us righteous who have put our faith in Jesus.

Our Rich Life in Christ   5:1-11

But what about our frail human nature? Is there any hope that we can be changed more and more perfectly into the spiritual image of Jesus Christ? Yes Paul replies, God's Holy Spirit pours his love into our hearts in such measure that all manner of godly fruit springs to life in our lives. We enjoy peace with God, a relation of total well-being (that is the sense of shalom [peace] in many places in the Old Testament). This peace of God so floods our hearts and lives that we can live victoriously even in tribulation. The Spirit fills us with hope, for we look forward gladly to the full salvation which the Lord will bring to his new covenant people in his glorious return from heaven.

Adam and Christ as Race Heads   5:12- Chap. 6

What a contrast there is, says Paul, between the old humanity in Adam and the new humanity in Christ! By his disobedience (the fall or revolt against God), Adam brought depravity (sin) and mortality (death) upon all humankind. But by his suffering obedience (becoming a sacrifice for sin on the cross of Gologtha), Christ brought just the opposite to his people: Righteousness and eternal life.

One with Christ in Death and New Life   Chap. 6

The secret of God's transforming power in the lives of those united with Christ is the way they are one with their Lord in identification with him in his death and resurrection. Romans 6 explains that we "co-die," we are "co-crucified" and "co-buried" with our Lord in order that we might "co-rise" with him! This is a dying to sin in the power of the Holy Spirit, and a "co-rising" to newness of life. This "co-dying" means that the body of sin might be "rendered powerless," for that is the exact meaning of the Greek verb which Paul uses about thirty-five times, and which is used also in Hebrews 2:14: the death of Christ as a sacrifice for sin "rendered powerless" the devil himself!

Victory Over Legalism and Depravity   7-8

Romans 7 sets forth the notion that the Christian is not a legalist, one in bondage to law; but in Christ one is set free to serve the Lord from love. Although still in the body with its weakness, moral and otherwise, all of which are frankly acknowledged, Christians have joyful hope in Christ, for it is he who is able to deliver them. The good ministry of the Holy Spirit is set forth at great length in Romans 8, which is one of the richest sections of the New Testament.

God and His Covenant People   9-11

Paul had a problem, a concern which caused his heart to ache: How could a loving and faithful God cast off many of his covenant people, that is Israel? For three chapters (9-11) Paul wrestles with this problem. He comes up with four comments: (1) God is both righteous and sovereign, and we mortals are in no position to challenge his goodness and justice. (2) It is Israel who did the rejecting, not God. (3) There is even yet a believing remnant in Israel; not all the children of the covenant are lost. (4) God wil yet show mercy to vast numbers of Israelites.

Disciples of Christ; Submissive Citizens; Considerate Church Members

Romans 12 is a splendid essay on the nature of the Christian life, the way people live who are made righteous and filled with the love which the Holy Spirit pours into their hearts. In the next chapter Christians are told to submit to the governing authorities in the state; and once more love is set forth as the fulfillment of the law of God. Romans 14 explains what it means to be a considerate member of the church—how a Christian does not live in disregard of the consciences of other Christians, even though those Christians may be in partial bondage to wrong convictions.

In Romans 15 Paul glories in the salvation of multitudes of Gentiles; here he shows that their conversion was clearly foretold by the Old Testament prophets. Jewish believers must accept this. In the last chapter there are greetings to Paul's many friends in the Roman church, and a plea to keep an eye on those who bring evil divisions into the congregation. The letter closes with the apostolic benediction and a beautiful doxology.

Some Translators on Romans

Luther Looks at Romans (Preface, 1532):

"This epistle is really the chief part of the New Testament and the very purest Gospel, and is worthy not only that every Christian should know it word for word, by heart, but occupy himself with it every day, as the daily bread of the soul. It can never be read or pondered too much, and the more it is dealt with the more precious it becomes, and the better it tastes"

(Martin Luther. *Commentary on the Epistle to the Romans* [Grand Rapids, Michigan: Kregel Publications] 1977, p. xiii).

Tyndale Endorses Luther (1534 Revised English New Testament):

"For as moche as this pistle is the principall & most excellent part of the newe testament, & most pure *Euagelion,* i.e., to say, Gladde tydings, & that we call Gospell, and also a lyghte & a way in unto the hole Scripture, I thynke it mete, that every Christian man not only knowe it by rote & withoute the boke, but also exercise him selfe therein evermore continually, as with the dayly brede of the soul. No man verely can read it to ofte or studie it to well: for the more it is studyed the easier it is, & the more groundely it is serched the preciouser things are found in it, so great treasure of spirituall things lyeth hyd therein."

May the Holy Spirit grant that those who read this commentary may have their attention directed to the text of the New Testament itself; may they find themselves drawn to (and not away from) this "most excellent part of the newe testament."

1

All People Need Deliverance
(Romans 1:1—3:20)

1:16-17   Key Verse

Prologue: 1:1-15

Greeting: 1:1-7

In the first century, writers of letters put down their own name first, then indicated to whom the letter was addressed, and finally gave a word of greeting (Acts 23:25-27). Paul follows contemporary practice. Since Rome was the center of the civilized world, a city estimated at a million inhabitants, Paul uses the universal language of the empire: *koine* Greek. This was not the sophisticated language of the classical Greek authors, but the everyday speech of common people. He also uses his Greek name Paul, rather than the Hebrew name Saul of his infancy and youth, the name which he probably used whenever he was in a Jewish community.

Paul calls himself a servant of Christ Jesus. The Greek word could well be rendered as slave. The word means that one belongs to an owner, that his will is that of the one to whom he belongs; Paul was very much a love slave of his Master. Perhaps we would get the force of the Greek better, especially in the minds of Paul's Jewish readers, if we entitled his Master, Messiah Jesus (for Messiah meant the anointed one in Hebrew; it is the exact equivalent of the Greek word "Christ").

24

Paul writes, conscious of the fact that his conversion to the Christian faith was a response to a divine summons. Indeed, turning to Jesus the Messiah in penitence and faith was the last thing he intended to do. Like C. S. Lewis of our day, Paul came into the kingdom "kicking." Prior to the divine call which he experienced near Damascus, Paul was a bitter opponent of "the way" (as the Christian faith and life are often described in the book of Acts). But when the Lord of glory addressed Saul in his mother tongue, the great apostle-to-be was physically blinded but spiritually illuminated, by the light from heaven. One could say he was overwhelmed by the impossible: Jesus of Nazareth is the "Son of man" who is also worthy of worship as the Son of God (Daniel 7:13, 14)! Each of the three accounts of the Damascus conversion experience has a few unique details (Acts 9, 22, 26).

God's ancient people, the Jews, had as their original heads the Twelve Patriarchs—the sons of Israel (Jacob); so also the Lord Jesus appointed twelve disciples to be the official witnesses of his resurrection, the leaders of the new Israel of God, and he named them apostles. Later, in a special revelation of himself, the Lord Jesus appeared to Paul also, so that he too was conscious of being an apostle, God confirmed Paul's apostleship by giving him miracle-working power (2 Corinthians 12:12). (In the New Testament, "apostle" is also sometimes used in a more general sense of those sent by God, such as Barnabas. See Acts 14:14.)

Paul saw himself as having been set apart, 'separated,' for the gospel, the good news of God. The good news is that in Christ there is forgiveness for penitent sinners. At times Paul did work as a tentmaker (Acts 18:3), but the real burden of his life, and his greatest joy, was to seek to lead people from a life of sin to repentance and faith in God's Messiah and Mediator, and to the "obedience of faith." Those characterized by repentance and faith are the people who give heed to God's good news, his gospel. And Paul saw the prophets foretelling the gospel in the Holy Scriptures.

For Paul, the good news centered in the Messiah, the Lord

Jesus. As to his human nature (the "flesh") Jesus was a Jew, a descendant of David whose kingdom was to stand forever (2 Samuel 7). And although truly human (the "Son of David"), he was also declared to be (designated as) the Son of God with power by the *Spirit of holiness,* that is by the Holy Spirit. The event which thus attested to the true deity of our Lord was his resurrection from the dead on that first Easter morning after the crucifixion. All the prophets of Israel, and all the apostles of Christ, stand around the Savior and witness: Lo, there is the one who became incarnate, who taught us about the kingdom of God, who died for our reconciliation with God and our spiritual victory over sin, who arose again in the body in which he suffered, who ascended to his Father, who is now enthroned at God's right hand, who intercedes for his human children, and who is coming again for them.

Paul refers to Jesus with two titles: First he is the Messiah (Christ) who was to come (this spoke loudly to the Jews); and then he is Lord or emperor *(kyrios).* The latter title spoke so loudly that it shocked the Gentiles, for it was the very term which they applied to the human head of the Roman Empire (and whose vanity sometimes caused him to call for worship of himself as a divine figure).

Now the purpose of Paul's call by God to a state of grace before God, and to the office of apostle in the church, was that he might bring many Gentiles to the obedience which saving faith results in: all this *for the sake of* Jesus' name! (How affirming these words must have been to the Gentile portion of the church in Rome!) And Paul was not the only believer God called to faith and obedience. The same Lord had also called every member of the Roman church to repentance and faith. Believers, says Paul (1:7), may be described in terms of privilege—as loved by God, and in terms of obligation—as called to be saints (holy ones). (As an adjective, the Greek word is translated holy, and as a substantive as saint; compare the German *heilig* and *Heiligen.*)

Paul concludes his prologue with the twin greetings of grace (similar to the common Greek greeting of the day) and peace (the

Hebrew greeting even today). But Christian content is poured into each of those words. Grace in the New Testament is infinitely richer than "Greetings!" It speaks of the marvel of us weak humans being fully accepted in the family of God without any merit in ourselves. And peace (the Hebrew shalom) is a state of total well-being, of fullness of blessing before God, including total reconciliation through the blood of Christ. Hallelujah!

Paul's Longing to Come to Rome: 1:8-15

Paul's first word after the prologue is one of thanksgiving to his God for every Christian believer at Rome. In common with the whole New Testament, prayer is addressed to God "through Jesus Christ," for we sinful human beings need a mediator. (Not mentioned here is the fact that real prayer is always "in the Spirit," that is, the Holy Spirit nudges each believer to prayer of adoration, intercession, thanksgiving, supplication.) Paul did not need to remind himself that he ought to give thanks for the Roman believers. Rather, when he observed how their faith was being reported all over the civilized Roman world, he was genuinely moved to thank God. Paul also declares that he served (or worshiped) God "in the spirit"—the verb here rendered *serve* is as a noun which is rendered *worship* in Hebrews 9:1. And to worship or serve "in the spirit" means to do so earnestly, "with the whole heart." The content of this service is defined as proclaiming the good news which centers in the mediator, Jesus Christ. Paul unceasingly entreated God to bless the Christians at Rome. Further Paul "begged" God to open the way for him to come to Rome. The verb for *come* hints at success, at things going well: "that I may have a happy journey," in other words.

Paul goes on to say that his longing to see the Roman Christians included the desire to bring to them a "spiritual gift" (cf. 12:6, gifts); that is, to see them made strong or established in the faith. But lest that sound too confident, he quickly adds: "that is, that you and I may be mutually encouraged [comforted] by each other's faith." (Several centuries ago the English word comfort could mean strengthen.) Paul had planned many times to go to

Rome, but something always got in his way. He had seen God pour out his blessings on Paul's ministry in the Gentile world so often that he was confident he would do it again among the Romans. Like Wesley, whose parish was the world, Paul burned with the desire to share the good news to both Jews and Gentiles, to those who were learned and to those of simple mind—the latter in the sense of those not yet illuminated by the Spirit of God.

The Theme: 1:16, 17

For I am not ashamed of the good news, declares the apostle, even though it centers in a man who died as a felon, for I know by experience that it brings a release of divine might to everyone who makes the surrender of faith. And this occurs regardless of race, to Jews as well as Greeks. For in the declaration of the good news is made known how to obtain the gift of divine righteousness: it comes from faith and in turn strengthens faith (trust). From first to last, it is a matter of giving up to Christ, of putting full trust in him. It is set forth forcibly in Holy Writ (Habakkuk 2:4). And here we come to the most glorious truth of God's Word: the very heart of the good news.

The great question of the sinner under conviction is: How may I become righteous before God? It is illustrated by the man fatally injured in a farm accident who, before he died, prayed: "O God, make me as pure as the angels!" But how can a mortal man become righteous before God? Habakkuk gives the answer. It is not a human achievement, it is not produced by good works, and it is not a matter of keeping God's law. Rather it is a gift of God. The Greek can be translated either of two ways:

"Now he who is righteous *by faith shall live."*

This was the rendering of Wyclif from the Latin about 1380: "The just shall live by faith." And it was so rendered in the Tyndale tradition: Tyndale, Tyndale-Coverdale, "Matthews," the Great Bible, Geneva, Bishops, King James, English Revised, and American Standard. But scholars as early as Beza (1519-1605,

Calvin's successor at Geneva) read the passage thus:

"Now he who is *righteous by faith* shall live."

And Beza was not giving a novel interpretation, for it had been so understood by Chrysostom (347-407), and it was also followed by Bengel (1687-1752). It is also supported by the Revised Standard Version, and by such outstanding commentators as Meyer (1800-1873) and Anders Nygren, the Swedish scholar (1944). It seems clear that Paul is not talking about how to *live* a genuine Christian life, but how to *become righteous* before God. He makes the point that it is not man's conformity to law, not man's own good works, but a sheer act of God's grace declaring the believer in Christ to possess the standing of perfect righteousness— not by works or by law, but through the surrender of faith. (We will return to this theme at Romans 3:21.)

All People Need the Gift of Divine Righteousness: 1:18—3:20

Gentile Sin and Need: 1:18-32   3-18-84

After announcing the theme of gift righteousness by which penitent believers may stand before God, fully reconciled with him through Christ, Paul suddenly turns to the theme of humankind's need of righteousness—in the Gentile world. With quick brushstrokes he paints a dark picture of human sin; he asserts that those who refuse the surrender of faith bring down upon themselves the wrath of God, a theme woefully lacking in contemporary Christendom. My senior professor at Westminster Theological Seminary, Oswald T. Allis, used to say that many people today think of God as a benign old grandfather who wouldn't kill a mosquito. But the Bible in general, and Christ in particular, took the sin of revolt against God, often called unbelief or disobedience in Scripture, very seriously. Sin is seen as intolerable to the holy eyes of God. Those who defy God's call to repentance are choosing the destiny of the devil and his angels (Matthew 25:46).

Paul therefore begins this section in 1:18 by declaring that the wrath of God is revealed against "un-piety" (impiety or god-lessness) and unrighteousness (wickedness) of people (*men* here is not males but representatives of humankind male or female). People hold back or suppress the truth by living in or defending unrighteousness. What does Paul mean when he accuses sinners of suppressing the truth? His next sentence clarifies his meaning. Sinners know better. God has revealed his power and his divinity (the fact that it is he who is God) by what he has made, the heavens and the earth. Sinners refuse to give glory to the Creator whose works speak loudly to those willing to listen (see Psalms 19 and 53).

Human stubbornness in three areas turns people away from the good Creator: (1) *Idolatry,* making images of the deity in the form of us poor mortals, or even like birds, animals, or reptiles. Paul says that people know better than that. (2) People take one of God's most beautiful creations, *human sexuality,* which he willed to be sanctified by the holy *agape love* of lifelong monog-amy, and in their moral "uncleanness" they stoop to vile affec-tions and ways of life. They prostitute God-given sex to practices condemned by the law of God, both men and women engaging in illicit relations with those of their own sex. Paul adds that they received back the proper penalty for their perversion: it is the penalty of shame, of the revulsion of holy men and women of God, not to mention the wrath of the Creator. He created sex for marriage, not for its perversion. (3) The final result of a wrong life is *sinful thinking,* even to the point of approving all manner of sinful acts. And so Romans 1 concludes with a long list of sins emanating from an evil, rebellious heart against God. God's worst judgment is not that of striking down people with illness or other calamities; it is the judicial hardening of God's holy law. Three times it is said: "God gave them over" (1:24, 26, 28). The law of sowing and reaping is God's law. God does not need to devise punishments for sin; sin brings its own evil harvest.

Future Judgment in the Hereafter: 2:1-16

By logic, one would expect Paul to conclude that people

who live by the law of God would surely have the right to be judgmental toward those who live in sin. But the word of Scripture is just the opposite: Do not judge others for their sins, because each human being has the same human nature, and in some measure is guilty of the same sins which he tends to condemn in others. Only God is able to assess guilt and to judge. And he will be absolutely holy and righteous in every judgment. Further, Christians must not forget how kind, tolerant, and patient God is with us fallible and weak human beings; this realization of God's kindness ought to move us to repentance.

As a matter of fact, human nature tends to be hard and impenitent; by nature we tend to try to get what we want instead of doing God's will. By such an attitude we "store up" against us the wrath of God for the day of his judgment. God will on that day give to each person a judgment suitable to the deeds of his life. There will be nothing arbitrary about the judgment of God. People will be judged according to their *relation to Christ.* There will be two classes on the day of judgment: (1) "To those who by persistent [endurance in this life] in doing good seek glory, honor and immortality [literally, incorruption], he [God] will give eternal life" (2:7). (2) But those guilty of living for recognition ("self-seeking"), who reject the demand of the good news to repent and surrender to Christ, those who "disobey" the truth of the gospel and "obey" unrighteousness: for these the day of judgment will bring divine wrath and anger. There will be trouble and distress for every human being who does evil—first for the Jews, then for the Gentiles. On the other hand, there will be glory, honor, and peace for everyone who does good, first for the Jews, then for the Gentiles ("Greeks"). For with God there is no favoritism; he is no respecter of persons.

We come then to those who never heard the law of God as revealed in the Holy Scriptures—the law of Moses and the writings of the prophets. Here the general principle holds: All those choosing to live in sin and defiance will perish whether or not they had heard the written law of God. For it is not those who were exposed to the Law (in the synagogue, for example) who will be seen as righteous before God, but those who obey what God asks for: they will be declared righteous (justified). There is a deep principle here: God's holy will, so clearly revealed in the written Law, is to some extent also mirrored in the human conscience; it is written on their hearts so that even the Gentiles can be obedient to the law of conscience. (People have guilt in so far as they have the light.) And this will become evident on the day when God will judge all people through Jesus Christ. This is part of the good news proclaimed by the "apostle to the Gentiles."

Jewish Sin and Need: 2:17—2:29

Paul now turns to his own people who were so prone to trust in their "Jewishness." They felt superior to the Gentiles because God had entrusted them with the Holy Scriptures (the Law, the Prophets, and the Psalms). They correctly held that they knew the will of God, and that they were therefore equipped to serve as spiritual guides, as lights in the midst of spiritual darkness. They were to be instructors for those who were ignorant of true wisdom, teachers of mere infants in divine matters; and obviously they felt a smug satisfaction in themselves. But Paul turns on them severely and asks: Do you live by those standards which you teach to those who have not the law of God? Do you ever steal? commit adultery? rob idol temples? You brag about the law, but do you then dishonor God who gave it by not keeping it? Let me tell you flat, says the apostle, it is through you Jews and your disobedience to God's law that the Gentiles blaspheme his holy name.

Circumcision, the sign of the holy covenant God made with Abraham, is of value in God's sight if, and only if, your life conforms to God's law. For if you are a breaker of God's law, you might as well skip circumcision. This means that when an uncircumcised Gentile is obedient to the law of God, he is reckoned as one of the covenant people, even though he lacks the physical sign of the covenant. Actually, he condemns you Jews who, though physically circumcised, do not live according to the holy law of God. All this means that you Jews have greater guilt, greater spiritual need, than the Gentiles, for you have more light because you have God's holy Word.

Being a Jew by race does not make one a member of the covenant people; it takes more than that. And it takes more than the sign of the covenant, circumcision. To really belong to God's people is to have received the circumcision of the heart so that you love God "with all your heart and with all your soul" (Deuteronomy 30:6). And such spiritual cleansing (circumcision) is the supernatural work of the Spirit of God. Law cannot effect a change of heart, but God's Spirit can. Get your eyes on God, the only one whose favor matters.

The Faithfulness of God: 3:1-8

Now if you Jews think that there are no advantages in being a Jew and in receiving circumcision, declares Paul, you have not understood me at all. Even if some Jews were not true children of the covenant, does that mean that the covenant was thereby destroyed? Of course not! God will still be true to his promises made to Abraham—even though people prove false! (Scripture explicitly supports this concept.)

Is it not true that the righteousness of God shines even more brightly in contrast with the darkness of our unrighteousness? Does the fact that God punishes our sin make him unrighteous? Not in the least! (Otherwise God could not qualify as our final judge!) Logic might claim: If my falsehood enhances the glory of God (by making his reliability even more striking), would this not excuse my sin? As a matter of fact, that very conclusion was being slanderously attributed to Paul himself; but it was not a truthful claim. Such slanderers deserve to be condemned!

All People Need Deliverance: 3:9-20

Paul begins to tighten his net of clear thinking about the sin and need of humankind. First, he concludes that the Jews are no better than the Gentiles (or "Greeks," as he calls them). Both Jews and Gentiles are sinners and need a deliverer. And he finds the Old Testament full of statements undergirding his conclusion. He quotes a total of seven statements from Psalms, Ecclesiastes, and Isaiah on the universality of sin in the human family. No one is in himself *righteous*. No one *seeks* God (apart from the wooing of God's Spirit.) People have *poisoned lips:* they slander and lie. Their feet are *swift to shed blood.* The *way of peace* they do *not know.* They have *no fear of God* before their eyes.

What is the sum total of this testimony? The answer is, *law cannot save sinners*. What law does is reveal God's righteous will and thereby it exposes the sin and need of every heart. It silences every mouth. Before God all humankind is guilty of sin. Observing the law will never lead to anyone being declared righteous. *Law cannot save.* If there is no Savior, humankind has only despair; there is no hope through moralism.

Reason to share: one beggar sharing
    with another beggar where he
    found bread - Ray

2

The Good News:
Righteousness by Faith

(Romans 3:21—3:31)

In the Greek language there is a family of words having to do with that which is righteous. There is the adjective *righteous,* a synonym for upright meaning that which is the opposite of sinful and evil. There is the noun *righteousness* which can describe those who are in a saving relation with God through Christ. Indeed, the Arndt-Gingrich *Greek-English Lexicon* speaks of the "righteousness bestowed by God," and adds: "In this area it closely approximates *salvation"* (p. 196). There is also an adverb, closely allied in form to the adjective, which refers to a manner of behaving uprightly or *righteously.* There are also nouns which can be rendered respectively as *righteous deed* and as *acquittal* or *justification.* But it is the verb which is especially meaningful in our study, and which is properly translated: *to pronounce righteous, to acquit, to justify,* or *to set free.* Unfortunately, English translations tend to vacillate between *righteous* and *just* for the adjective, to use *righteousness* or *justification* for the nouns, and to use *justify* for the verb. The words on the *righteous* stem derive from Old English, while those on the *just* stem derive ultimately from the Latin. To preserve better Paul's chain of thought, the Old English words *righteous, righteousness,* and to *declare righteous,* etc., will be used here.

Gift Righteousness: 3:21-31

Now Available in Christ: 3:21.

Paul writes specifically, "But now a righteousness ... has been made known." The *now* has temporal force. It means in this Christian era, this period since Good Friday, Easter morning, and Pentecost. The only righteousness which really avails before God is that which he gives. And he gives it only to those who are "in Christ." It is always an undeserved gift, never a matter of personal achievement. The Jews failed to heed the good news so that they disregarded the gift-righteousness which comes from God and sought to achieve their own. They simply did not submit to God, and thus receive the divine gift of righteousness (see Romans 10:3).

After Paul was converted, in contrast with the non-Christian Jews, Paul could write that he does not have "a righteousness of my own that comes from the law, but that which is through faith in Christ—the righteousness that comes from God and is by faith" (Phil. 3:9).

Our Lord one time urged the Jews to work for the food "that endures to eternal life." Quick as a flash the Jews asked: "What must we do to do the works God requires?" Jesus replied simply, "The work of God is this: to believe in the one he has sent" (John 6:27-29).

Affirmed in Holy Writ: 3:21

Romans, Philippians, and *John* were all written after Pentecost, of course. But Paul is quite bold: he asserts that the doctrine of gift-righteousness was taught even by "the Law and the Prophets." As a matter of fact, Paul appeals explicitly to three passages. (1) As we saw in 1:17, Paul quoted the Greek Old Testament, the Septuagint (made about 285-135 BC): "The righteous will live by faith" (that is, shall enjoy real life, "eternal life"). (2) In Romans 4:3 Paul quotes Genesis 15:6, referring to the "father of the faithful": "Abram believed the Lord, and he credited it to him as righteousness." (We will look at this more closely in the next chapter in which Paul does a case study of this Old Testament man of faith in support of his doctrine of gift-righteousness.) (3) Finally, Paul quotes Psalm 32:1, 2, as follows (Romans 4:7, 8):

> Blessed are they
>   whose transgressions are forgiven,
>   whose sins are covered.
> Blessed is the man
>   whose sin the Lord will never
>   count against him.

(In the original Hebrew [of Psalm 32] the word Lord is called the *tetragrammaton,* the name of the covenant God of Israel, printed in many Bibles as four capital letters, including the King James and New International versions. In the Hebrew it is written something like JHWH, and was probably pronounced *Yahweh;* at least many scholars make this conjecture.)

Those Who Receive Gift-Righteousness: 3:22

The righteousness of the one in Christ is described as the gift-righteousness of God. During the Middle Ages people had lost sight of this aspect of the good news and had often come to think of righteousness as a human achievement. The "faithful" tried to bring before God all their works of merit. For ordinary mortals this included prayer, alms, fasting, and the like. The spiritually elite also renounced the holding of personal property, denied themselves the joys of living with a spouse, and promised to render absolute obedience to the head of their monastic order. A good example of such a monk was Martin Luther (c.1483-1546). He himself said later that if self-denial and good works of all kinds could have brought anyone to heaven, he would have been successful, for he was so severe with himself that he endangered his health. But the route of self-denial for its own sake, and the doing of works which supposedly achieved merit, simply could not bring the scholarly and devout monk of Wittenberg to peace and joy. His fellowmonks could not understand or help him, nor could the learned Professor von Staupitz of his university.

It happened one day (possibly in 1514) that Luther was sitting in deep thought. Somehow he happened to settle on Romans 1:17 which states that the righteousness of God is revealed in the gospel and that it is *obtained by faith. By faith,* thought Luther: then it is not a quality in the holy God by which he punishes us poor mortals! By faith! *Righteousness by faith!* Luther was overwhelmed. In describing the scene later, Luther could only say that it was the Holy Spirit who illuminated him in the tower of the Black Monastery in Wittenberg. He says that it was as if he had been born again! In fact, this recovery of the Good News, which had been largely lost for a thousand years, was the most basic foundation principle of the great sixteenth-century Reformation. Luther called this truth of righteousness by faith by the Latin word *justificatio* (justification by faith, in English).

Paul here indicates that the righteousness of God is given to those who put their faith in Christ—it is given to all those who believe. Away, therefore, with any thought of good works as a means of earning merit before God! Much more, works of "supererogation" (additional works not required for salvation) are abolished.

Sin and Need Universal: 3:23

Paul looked back over history and declared: All people have sinned. That is, they all needed a mediator with God. They all needed a sin offering. Then Paul looked around at his contemporaries and observed: All of them are falling short, also! (The first verb refers to the past; the second to the present.) People ought to live only for the glory of God. Someone has said that to glorify God we need to be persons through whom others come to understand God better and appreciate him more. Measured by such a standard, all people fall short. Sin and need are universal.

The apostle John taught exactly the same doctrine as Paul. "If we claim to be without sin," John wrote, "we deceive ourselves and the truth is not in us. If we confess our sins, he is faithful and [righteous] . . . and will forgive us our sins and purify us from all unrighteousness" (1 John 1:8, 9).

To a sick Christian woman, Griet Edes, Menno Simons wrote: "I understand that your conscience is troubled because you have not and do not walk in such perfection as the Scriptures hold before us. I write the following to my faithful sister as a brotherly consolation from the true Word and eternal truth of the Lord. The Scripture, says Paul, has concluded all under sin. There is no man on earth, says Solomon, who does righteously and sinneth not. At another place: A just man falleth seven times, and riseth up again. Moses says: The Lord, the merciful God, merciful and gracious, longsuffering and abundant in goodness and truth, keeping mercy for thousands, forgiving iniquity and transgression and sin. O dear sister, notice, he says, None are without sin before God. And David says, Lord, enter not into judgment with thy servant; for in thy sight shall no [person] living be justified. And we read, If they sin against thee (for there is no man that sinneth not). We are all as an unclean thing, and all our righteousness is as filthy rags. Christ also said, There is none good but one, that is God. The evil which I would not, that I do. In many things we all offend. If we say that we have no sin, we deceive ourselves, and the truth is not in us.

"Since it is plain from all these Scriptures that we must all confess ourselves to be sinners, as we are in fact; and since no one under heaven has perfectly fulfilled the righteousness required of God but Christ Jesus alone; therefore none can approach God, obtain grace, and be saved, except by the perfect righteousness, atonement, and intercession of Jesus Christ, however godly, righteous, holy, and unblamable he may be. We must all acknowledge, whoever we are, that we are sinners in thought, word, and deed. Yes, if we did not have the righteous Christ Jesus, no prophet nor apostle could be saved.

". . . You can expect no greater righteousness in yourself than all the chosen of God had in them from the beginning. In and by yourself you are a poor sinner, and by the eternal righteousness banished, accursed, and condemned to eternal death." (*Writings,* pp. 1052-1053).

Righteousness from God a Gift: 3:24

Paul almost exulted as he wrote that we are "declared righteous" by the grace of God. Many versions add to the first phrase, *freely.* But the word freely is hardly adequate to convey the meaning intended. Freely can mean in as large amounts as desired. But Paul says that we are declared righteous as a gift. Revelation 21:6 promises the spiritually thirsty person: "I will give to drink without cost [as a gift] from the spring of the water of life." And one of the most beautiful gospel invitations of Scripture is found in Revelation 22:17: "The Spirit and the bride say, 'Come!' And let him who hears say, 'Come!' Whoever is thirsty, let him come; and whoever wishes, let him take the free gift of the water of life." (The same Greek word is used in Romans 3:24, Revelation 21:6, and Revelation 22:17.)

As a matter of fact, the meaning would be there even without the phrase, "as a gift," for Paul indicates that we are "declared righteous ... by his grace." What is by grace is not earned, paid for, or deserved. It is simply ours by the utter generosity of the giver. But when *as a gift* or *without cost* is added, the overwhelming character of gift righteousness is emphasized.

Now this gift of righteousness has been made possible by Christ's redemption. To help us grasp the adequacy of his offering for our sins on Golgotha's cross, the New Testament employs three expressions: (1) we are redeemed by the blood of Christ, which is used in Ephesians 1:7 (and ninety-four other references!); (2) we are redeemed through the death of Christ, as in Romans 5:10 and Hebrews 2:9; and (3) we are redeemed by the cross of Christ, as in Colossians 1:20. All three expressions point to the same redemption, the same reconciliation with the Father, accomplished by the sacrifice Christ offered to God on Golgotha. The remarkable thing about Christ our great high priest is that he offered himself as a sin offering on the cross of Golgotha (Hebrews 7:27; 9:14; 9:26). Animal sacrifices under the old covenant could never atone for sin (Hebrews 10:4).

Menno therefore continued in his letter to Griet Edes: "It is a very precious word which Paul speaks, When we were yet without strength, in due time Christ died for the ungodly. Yea, when we were yet ungodly, and thereby He manifests His love toward us. For if, when we were enemies, we were reconciled to God by the death of His Son, much more, being reconciled, we shall be saved by His life. . . .

"I pray and desire that you will betake yourself wholly both as to what is inward and what is outward unto Christ Jesus and His merits, believing and confessing that His precious blood alone is your cleansing; His righteousness your piety; His death your life; and His resurrection your justification; for He is the forgiveness of all your sins; His bloody wounds are your reconciliation; and His victorious strength is the staff and consolation of your weakness. . . ." (*Writings*, p. 1053).

Our Mercy Seat: 3:25, 26

Paul continues this exposition of divine righteousness as a gift by pointing out that God presented Christ as a *propitiation* (see KJV). There is no question but that the Greek word may legitimately be translated as *propitiation* or *expiation* (see RSV). But New Testament scholars are deeply impressed with how much the Greek Old Testament (the Septuagint) influenced the thinking and the vocabulary of the Greek New Testament writers. Luther was a splendid translator. And since the Greek Old Testament used this very word for the lid of the ark (the "mercy seat" on which the blood of expiation was ceremonially sprinkled on the most holy Day of Atonement by the high priest), Luther therefore translated *propitiation* by its Septuagint meaning as *Gnadenstuhl* (mercy seat). And Tyndale, who started the tradition which we have in the ERV, ASV, RSV, NASV, and the New KJV, rendered the word *seat of mercy*. (Later revisers changed it.) The same word occurs in Hebrews 9:5 (a book which draws innumerable parallels between the Jewish priesthood, sacrifices, ceremonies, and tabernacle and their ultimate fulfill-

ment in Christ and his redemption) where it may also legitimately be translated as *mercy seat* (see Arndt-Gingrich, p. 376).

Just as there had to be shed blood and a forfeited life for the
ceremony related to the forgiveness of sin in the Mosaic law,
including a *mercy seat* between the broken law of God and
Jahweh himself, so Christ is the *"mercy seat"* between his failing
disciples and the holy God of heaven. Our hope of forgiveness
and eternal life lies in his shed blood, in the giving of his life for
us on the cross of Golgotha, in the sin offering he presented to
the Father.

The Cross and God's Righteousness

In the midst of a long Greek sentence, Paul suddenly remarks that the offering of Jesus for our reconciliation
demonstrated God's righteousness. He explains that God had
been so indulgent with sin prior to Golgotha, he had so often
seemed to overlook sin, that his very righteousness could con-
ceivably have been called into question. But on that Good Friday, when our Lord died in shame and suffering, God made
clear that sin is an awful reality and that it does call for a costly,
propitiatory "mercy seat." Sin was so awful that it cost the life of
the Son of God. The cross therefore reveals both the love of God
for us sinners and the full righteousness of God. Humankind
now knows that God is himself righteous, as well as that he
declares righteous the person who puts his faith in Jesus, our
perfect example, and the lamb of God.

No Human Boasting: 3:27-31

People are utterly prone to be self-willed and proud. The
worst form of pride is self-satisfaction, even conceit, over one's
attainments in character and service. Paul is entirely realistic
when he asks, "In view of God's plan of salvation by gift
righteousness, given lavishly to those in Christ, what place is
there for boasting, for pride of human achievement?" The
answer is really devastating. Since salvation is wholly the gift of
God, there is no place at all for human pride. For salvation does

not come through human achievement: neither in Christlikeness of character nor in effectiveness of service. No form of legalism can enable sinful people to attain heaven. Salvation is wholly of divine grace; it is given to those who know that they have nothing at all to offer to God as payment for a place in heaven. This applies just as much to the Jews, those who by divine love and grace had been God's special people to give to the world the holy scriptures and the Savior, as to the Gentiles.

Christians "keep" the law of God, not out of legalism, but because they love God from the heart (Deuteronomy 6:5). They follow Christ who fulfilled the law. They live above law, desiring the best for all people, including their salvation and deliverance from sin and its consequences. Indeed James, our Lord's half-brother (not James the son of Zebedee), speaks of living by the "royal law," loving your neighbor as yourself (Leviticus 19:18). It is this principle, and only this, which lifts people above legalism into the delightful realm which is appropriately called freedom (James 2:12). Freedom is not liberty to follow the world, the flesh, or the devil: it is rather the glorious privilege of being filled with agape love through the blessed ministry of the Spirit with whom each believer is baptized by Christ at conversion (Acts 1:5; 2:4; 11:15; 1 Corinthians 12:13; Romans 8:9).

Under the old covenant a person was born into the covenant people by natural birth; the sign of the covenant was given to each Jewish boy on the eighth day (as it was with Paul: Philippians 3:5). Each Jewish child was a part of the people of privilege and had opportunity to know the law and the God who had given it, for it was to the Jews that God had entrusted "the very words (oracles) of God" (Romans 3:2). Israel's election was not due to their merit, but to the exceeding great love of God (Deuteronomy 7:7-11). But human nature is such that the Jews were tempted to substitute the concept of their own innate superiority to the Gentiles for the biblical concept of the amazing love of God for them.

The Gentiles could, of course, boast of their sculptors, painters, philosophers, and world leaders, but neither art nor philosophy could bring people to God and his salvation. (This thought is developed well in 1 Corinthians 2:18-25.)

But all people, whether Jews or Gentiles, have but one way to God's salvation: it is the way of the Good News, namely, that God so loved the world that he had his only Son become incarnate as a true human being; Christ walked among us and taught us, fulfilling the Laws demands for us; God allowed the Romans to crucify him on the cross of Golgotha, where he suffered and died as the lamb of Isaiah 53; God raised him from the dead on the third day; and after forty days of further teaching of his disciples, he ascended to glory where he was enthroned as our mediator at the right hand of the Father. In response to the good news, with its call to repentance and surrender, both believing Jews and believing Gentiles are cleansed from sin; they are born into the family of God by the birth which is from above; they become joyful, forgiven, and transformed children of God; they walk in Christian freedom in the power of the Spirit; they put no confidence in self and in human achievement; and they are in a state of full acceptance by the Father because of his free gift of righteousness. Hallelujah!

It is such born again people, and only they, who truly keep the law of God. They are able in the power of the Spirit to uphold (not nullify) God's holy law. (Later in the letter, Paul discusses at length how Spirit-filled disciples live.)

3

Abraham, Father
of Believers

(Romans 4)

Who Was Abraham?

About 2,000 BC there lived in ancient Sumer (later Babylonia, now Iraq) a man by the name of Abram, whose name was later changed by God to Abraham. His town was called Ur; it was a site for the worship of the moon-god Nannar and his wife, Ningal. Ur was located on the west bank of the Euphrates and was settled many centuries before the time of Terah, Abraham's father. Ur contained a ziggurat (tower) in honor of the moon-god, and was a highly civilized city for that time. Abraham's ancestors were idolaters. In the course of time, however, Abraham worshiped only the God of heaven, the one who had made heaven and earth and all the hosts of heaven. It may be that Abraham had some knowledge of the true faith which had been held by such ancient persons as Seth, Enoch, and Noah, but the most important factor in bringing him to monotheism was the direct revelation he received from God on various occasions.

At an unknown date, Abraham, who had married his half-sister Sarai (later Sarah), left Ur, along with his father Terah and other relatives, and migrated northwestward toward Canaan. As a matter of fact, the people who made that journey in those days followed a large semicircle around the huge desert of Arabia; this semicircle extended from ancient Babylonia all the way to Canaan, and even to Egypt—a distance of perhaps a thousand miles around this "Fertile Crescent." But Terah, Abraham, and party went only as far as Haran, some distance east of the Euphrates and directly east of the northeast corner of the Mediterranean Sea. Haran was a good halfway to Canaan, and was located in an area called Paddan-Aram, between the Euphrates and the Tigris rivers. Haran was also a city devoted to the moon-god. There Abraham remained until the death of his father; then he migrated on to Canaan. When he left Haran, Abraham was seventy-five years of age.

The Pilgrim

Abraham lived as a pilgrim in Palestine, residing in tents; this was in great contrast to his earlier life. Mention is made of his living at Bethel, Shechem, the Oaks of Mamre, Hebron, and Beersheba. Many years he lived in the Negev, the "south country" of Canaan. Because of a famine he also sojourned in Egypt for a time. What really stands out in Abraham's life is the way God revealed himself to him. Abraham had moved to Canaan by direction of the Lord (Genesis 12:1). God promised the land of Canaan to Abraham's posterity (Genesis 12:7; 13:15); and he assured Abraham that he and Sarah would have a son and through him he would be the father of a vast people (Genesis 15:1-6). In this connection, special mention is made of the fact that "Abraham believed the Lord," his covenant God (15:6). Special mention is also made of a theophany (divine appearance) in connection with the Abrahamic covenant (15:17-20). The sign of the covenant was an ancient practice called circumcision (17:1-14). Before the divine destruction of four of the cities of the plain (Sodom, Gomorrah, Admah, and Zeboiim) near the south end of the Salt (Dead) Sea, the Lord again revealed himself and his imminent judgment to Abraham (19:1-29). When God tested Abraham as to whether he loved God enough to offer Isaac as a burnt offering, Abraham in faith obeyed God; God then countermanded the order and promised great blessings to Abraham; he added a promise that through Abraham's "seed" all nations would be blessed (22:15-18). The New Testament sees in this promise a reference to the Lord Jesus Christ (Galatians 3:16). Abraham finally died at the age of 175; his sons Isaac (Sarah's son) and Ishmael (Hagar's son) laid his body to rest beside that of Sarah's in the cave of Machpelah near Mamre, the town or district of modern Hebron.

Abraham came to be thought of in the Judeo-Christian tradition as a symbol of faith in God. The book of Galatians asserts that those who believe are "children of Abraham." Abraham himself is called "the man of faith" (Galatians 3:6-9). No wonder then that Paul devotes all of Romans 4 to the "father of those who believe." This brings us then to the crucial question: What was it in Abraham that made him acceptable to God?

Abraham Righteous by Faith—Not by Good Works

Was Abraham Declared Righteous Because of His Good Life? Romans 4:1-8

Paul cited Habakkuk 2:4 in Romans 1:17. Now he turns to his second supportive statement from the "Oracles of God," Genesis 15:6. This was given on the occasion when God promised Abraham that he and barren Sarah would in due time become the parents of a son who would be the father of a vast people: Abraham believed the word of the Lord, who credited it to him as righteousness. Paul is asking his Roman readers to think about that statement. Was Abraham regarded as righteous because of his righteous life of good deeds? No, says the Scripture. Abraham's trust in the faithfulness and reliability of the word of the covenant God, the Lord, led to an obedient life.

When a man works for wages, his payment is not a gift; the employer pays the wages because they have been earned. Wages are not a matter of grace! But when a person sees himself impious or wicked, yet, like Abraham of old, puts his whole confidence in the God who is the source of the good news his faith is credited as righteousness (Romans 4:5).

This brings Paul to his third Scripture text in support of gift-righteousness. In Romans 4:7, 8 he quotes David from Psalm 32:1, 2 who is here rejoicing in the divine forgiveness of the person who transgresses; such an individual is also a person of faith, for David asserts that the Lord will never count his sin against him!

Not by Ceremony

Was Abraham Declared Righteous Because of Rite or Ceremony? 4:9-12

It would seem reasonable enough for a religious person to think that Abraham was after all pronounced righteous because he bore in his body the mark of the holy covenant with Yahweh, Israel's covenant God. The symbol of that covenant, given by God himself, was the sacred rite of circumcision. But hold on, cries Paul, you are misreading the Bible! For the pronouncing of Abraham as being "righteous by faith" occurred in Genesis 15:6, whereas Abraham was not circumcised until much later (Genesis 17:24). No ceremony, despite its symbolic richness, can give a person perfect status with God. Only faith can cause one to be pronounced righteous, the basis for the obedient life (1:5; 15:18; 16:26). Abraham's circumcision, says Paul, was "a seal of the righteousness that he had by faith while he was still uncircumcised" (4:11). Religious ceremonies have real value for those who have saving faith in Christ. But they are never substitutes for faith.

At this point, Paul has to put in a word for his Gentile readers at Rome. Abraham, he says, is the spiritual father of all who believe but have not been circumcised. These believers, even though not circumcised, will also have righteousness credited to them. And then with his characteristically large heart, he also puts in a good word for his fellow Jewish believers. Abraham is also their father, he writes, for they are not only circumcised, but they also walk in the footsteps of the faith of Abraham, the faith he had *before* he was circumcised!

Not by Law

Was Abraham Declared Righteous on the Basis of His Having Observed the Law? 4:13-17.

In Romans 4:2 we saw that Abraham was not declared righteous because of his good works. In 4:9 we saw that he did not receive gift righteousness by ceremony (that is, by circumcision). Now Paul considers a third possibility: Could it be that Abraham kept the holy law of God so carefully that it pleased God, who thereupon "credited it to him as righteousness?" No, says Paul once again, we simply have to stick to the text: "Abraham believed the Lord, and he credited it to him as righteousness" (Genesis 15:6). Abraham's perfect standing before God came through the righteousness that comes by faith! All that law can do is to bring upon sinners the wrath of God. And then Paul drops a most significant remark: "Where there is no law there is no transgression." That is, people have guilt only to the extent that they know the law of God, to the extent that they have the light. Guilt is commensurate with light.

The God of the Impossible

No matter how often we go around and around, says Paul, we always come out at the same place. It is those who have faith who can claim the promise of gift righteousness—conformity to Christ in character and life. And this includes all the people of God: first, the believing Jews (those of the law) and those who have Abraham's faith (believing Gentiles). Paul looks upon the church as consisting of believers from many nations, and that situation fulfills the divine word to Abraham that he would be the father of many nations. Furthermore, Abraham's God was the one who does miracles: He gives life to the dead—as Abraham confidently expected God to raise up Isaac after he was slain by his father on Mount Moriah. God had told Abraham to offer up Isaac. So being certain that God would not break his promise that through Isaac Abraham would have a vast progeny, "Abraham reasoned that God could raise the dead, and figuratively

speaking, he did receive Isaac back from death" (Hebrews 11:19).
This God of miracles also calls things that are not as though
they were. To God there are no impossibilities. If he wishes an
Isaac to be born, the aged Abraham and Sarah become parents.
If he wishes Abraham to be the father of many nations, the many
families of Abraham's sons will be "created" by the one who is
sovereign: Ishmael and Isaac, as well as Keturah's sons: Zimran,
Jokshan, Medan, Midian, Ishbak, and Shuah (Genesis 25:2).
Nothing is impossible for God; he is able to do as he wills. In
Daniel 4:35 we read:

> He does as He pleases
>   with the powers of heaven
>   and the peoples of the earth.
> No one can hold back his hand
>   or say to him: "What have you done?"

What Is the Nature of Saving Faith? 4:18-25

God had given his word that Sarah should bear a son to
Abraham, the son of the divine promise. And yet one decade
after another rolled around, and no child came. No wonder then
that the Bible says that Abraham believed against all hope. Apart
from the omnipotent power of God, the case was hopeless. In his
human weakness it must have been difficult for Abraham.
"Could I have misunderstood what God intended?" he must
have pondered. And yet, in the end, Abraham always came out
on the side of faith. In hope he believed. As always, God
honored the faith of his son; as always he kept his word. Romans
4:19 indicates the two sides, both of which seemed real: on the
one hand, Abraham faced the fact that in his own body, at the
approximate age of a hundred, his body was as good as dead; as
far as Sarah was concerned, humanly there was no hope of a son
at all. Yet God had promised! And Abraham clung to his faith in
God's faithfulness, his utter reliability. Abraham did not give up.
Rather he was strengthened in his faith. The Arndt-Gingrich
Greek *Lexicon* suggests that in this passage it means that Abra-

ham grew strong in his faith. And yet since the passive voice is used, the NIV is more likely correct: Abraham was strengthened, which can only mean that the Spirit of God kept nourishing him in the inner man so that his faith did not grow weak, or even die. Abraham kept on trusting. He did not look at circumstances; his eye was on God. And most remarkably, he gave glory to God. When he thought of the divine promise as he rested during the heat of the day, or as he meditated under the stars at night, he murmured to God: "Thank you, O Father, for the promise! All glory be to you, O God, for the son you will yet give to Sarah and me!"

God Is Sovereign

The explanation for this unusual trust is clear. Abraham believed that God had power to do what he had promised. George Muller (1805-1898), of the Bristol, England, orphanage fame, became famous for the many answers God gave to his prayers. In fact, he tabulated 30,000 such answers. But he also admits that for many decades he had prayed for a certain thing, something he felt was in line with the will of God, and yet it did not come. At times, says Muller, his confidence that God would give the blessing became so great that he thanked God in advance for the gift, and even gave him glory for granting it. This is the struggle of faith. Why does God sometimes seem so slow? Why must peoples such as the American Indians or the blacks wait interminably for full justice? The Harvard poet James Russell Lowell (1819-1891) wrote:

> Careless seems the great Avenger; history's pages but record
> One death-grapple in the darkness 'twixt old systems and the
>   Word;
> Truth forever on the scaffold, Wrong forever on the throne—
> Yet that scaffold sways the future, and, behind the dim unknown,
> Standeth God within the shadow, keeping watch above his own.

Abraham did not hold to the "quickie" theory of Christianity: quickie holiness, quickie maturity, quickie answers to prayer: his faith had in it a staying quality. Abraham's quiet faith won the divine word: Abraham is righteous in my sight because of his faith! And this glorious declaration applies to us who believe in him who raised our Lord from the dead. Most of us are never granted to see the risen Christ, but we claim the promise: "Blessed are those who have not seen and yet have believed" (John 20:29).

Paul concludes his case study with a summary statement on the object of Christian faith: *He was delivered over to death for our sins.* This reflects Isaiah's prophecy of Jahweh's suffering servant (Isaiah 53). Peter summarized the idea this way: "He himself bore [literally carried up] our sins in his body on the tree [the cross] . . . by his wounds you have been healed" (1 Peter 2:24). Paul adds, finally, that he "was raised to life for our justification"—that is, that we might possess gift-righteousness. (The Greek word means the state of those who have been *declared righteous by faith.*) Faith lays hold on all the blessings of being in Christ.

4

The Fruit of Faith in Christ
(Romans 5)

The Chain of Faith: 5:1-5

Therefore, since we have been declared righteous by faith—
this is the central emphasis in the New Testament doctrine of salvation. And we have just seen that this righteousness does not come by works (4:2), by ceremony (4:9), or by law (4:13). Our perfect standing with the Father is a result of his goodwill toward those who, by faith, are "in Christ." *We have peace with God.* This is the reading adopted by the United Bible Societies' text, as well as by the NIV translators. There is strong manuscript evidence, however, that it should read: "Let us have peace with God." If this is correct (and John Murray calls the manuscript evidence "formidable"), the meaning is: *Let us go on enjoying* this state of "peace," of full acceptance, of total well-being with the Father. Meyer and R. C. H. Lenski both support the hortatory reading ("Let us"), but not in the sense of earning or meriting this acceptance with God; the whole context demolishes such views decisively, for this peace is ours through our Lord Jesus Christ. Then Paul adds, "through whom we have gained access [and this access is not by merit but *by faith*] into this grace in which we now stand." Since being declared righteous is the sure fruit of surrender to Christ, it is the full reality of the new believer

just as much as that of the seasoned soldier of the cross. It is the possession of the believing teenager just as much as the aged man or woman in Christ. All believers stand in grace.

Menno Simons wrote well: "Tell me, who is it that is circumcised with the circumcision of Christ? Is it not the believer? Who is it that has put off the body of sin by the circumcision of Christ?. . . We are all accepted into the covenant with God, not by any signs [ceremonies] but by grace . . . (for if it were by the signs, it would not be by grace)" (*Writings,* p. 261).

"And we rejoice [boast] in the hope of the glory of God" (5:2). The Greek word for boast refers, as John Murray so aptly puts it, to "exultant rejoicing and confident glorying." It is the holy confidence and joy of being a full child of God, and this joyful assurance is the right of every believer, young or old, immature or more Christlike, in character. This hope is not exhausted in this life but extends into the hereafter: "In the city of God, in the new Jerusalem, there we will await each other, before the throne of God and of the Lamb, sing Hallelujah, and praise His name in perfect joy" (Menno, *Writings,* p. 1054).

Paul goes on: "We also rejoice [boast] in our sufferings" (5:3) or tribulations. Paul elsewhere describes in some detail what it cost him to be a disciple of Jesus: imprisonment, floggings, lashings, beatings, stonings, lack of sleep, hunger, thirst, inadequate clothing (2 Corinthians 11:23-29). And he was also keenly aware that in this life we remain in a body of humiliation, we still have "lowly bodies" (Philippians 3:21), but our redemption in Christ also includes incorruptible "resurrection bodies" (1 Corinthians 15:35-55). Salvation in Christ will, at his return, include "the redemption of our bodies" (Romans 8:23). Meanwhile, God also worked miracles of healing through the hands of Paul (2 Corinthians 12:12; Acts 19:12), although such healings still left those who were healed in their lowly, unredeemed bodies.

"Suffering produces [works out] perseverance" (5:3). The fruit of suffering for Christ is not a spineless patience which makes one content to sit in a rocking chair all day. It is rather like a seasoned soldier of Christ who may flee to the highlands of Galatia, perhaps in the hope of getting rid of some illness such as malaria (see Galatians 4:13, 14). Prisoners of Christ who are interned for years without citrus fruit may develop scurvy. Prisoners who are beaten may suffer broken bones which may heal in misshapen forms. But regardless of what suffering disciples may be called upon to endure, they may grow stronger in faith and victorious joy all the while. "Blessed [or happy] are those who are persecuted because of righteousness, for theirs is the kingdom of heaven" (Matthew 5:10). "We must go through many hardships [afflictions] to enter the kingdom of God" (Acts 14:22). The apostles of Christ did not teach the modern theory of a crown earned without a cross. An old German hymn expresses well the New Testament theology of the believer's cross:

> Every Christian heareth gladly
> of the glorious kingdom fair,
> For they think that from afar
> it already is prepared.
> But whene'er they hear it said
> that Christ's cross one has to bear
> His disciple to be truly,
> ah, how few there are who come!
>
> Good it sounds whene'er 'tis said,
> All those burdened come to me,
> But 'tis a doctrine quite severe:
> Enter through the narrow door!
> When one hears Hosannas ringing,
> sweet it sounds to every ear.
> But when one heareth, Crucify!
> Every one therefrom doth flee.
> —*Zions Harfe,* 194

"Perseverance [produces] character" (5:4). There is only one way to attain Christian maturity of character: it calls for one to walk in love, holiness, and obedience—not in human strength, but in the power of God's Holy Spirit. We develop the right kind of character by deciding moment by moment not to walk according to the "flesh," but according to the leading of the Spirit of

God. As a somewhat immature disciple of our Lord, Peter could cringe in fear before the accusing remark of a maid-servant, "You also were with that Nazarene, Jesus" (Mark 14:67). But after he had walked for decades in Holy Spirit obedience, legend has it that he refused to be crucified as was his Lord; he insisted on being crucified head downward! Persevering in holy obedience produces character.

"Character [produces] hope" (5:4). Today we use the word hope for that which is totally uncertain: "I hope my old car will run another hundred thousand miles." But in the New Testament, hope is dynamic. It is a glorious reality. Paul had the hope of the "resurrection of the dead" (Acts 23:6). Christians have the hope that the creation itself will be liberated and will enter the freedom of the children of God (Romans 8:21). When we have Christian hope, we are able to wait patiently (Romans 8:25). Ultimately our hope is in heaven (Colossians 1:5). Because Christ dwells in us, we have the hope of reaching the glory world (Colossians 1:27). The Christian hope par excellence is the promise that Christ is coming again: this is "the hope of glory" (Colossians 1:27). The hope that God will bless us with perseverance is an "anchor for the soul" (Hebrews 6:19). All this means that the longer we walk with the Lord, the more sure is our confidence in his faithfulness, goodness, and keeping power.

"Hope does not disappoint us, because God has poured out his love into our hearts" (5:5). Jesus taught us that the greatest commandment in God's gracious instruction, the holy Torah (Law), was love for God and love for man (Matthew 22:35-40). Jesus, therefore, put such emphasis on the foundational character of love that he called it his "new commandment" (John 13:34). To "carry each other's burdens" is to "fulfill the law of Christ" (Galatians 6:2)—a clear reference to John 15:12: "My command is this: Love each other as I have loved you." And the New Testament tells us plainly that to love God is to obey his commands (1 John 5:2).

But the question has to be faced: How can we fallible children of Adam love God with all our heart, soul, and mind?

The answer of God's Holy Word is clear. As a part of his glorious offer of redemption in Christ, as an aspect of what we call "Christian experience," God pours his love into our hearts. Such divine love is therefore not a human achievement. It is a divine gift, just as are all other aspects of being saved. All these good gifts are the "fruit of the Spirit" (Galatians 5:22, 23). This is another way of saying that God "baptizes" us with his Spirit, or God "gives" us his Spirit. Another phrase is, God "pours out" his Spirit, or the Spirit "fell upon" us. So our text puts it succinctly: "God has poured out his love into our hearts by the Holy Spirit, whom he has given us" (5:5). All Christians have the Spirit (Romans 8:9).

Christ as Our Reconciler: 5:6-8

"You see [or indeed], at just the right time, when we were still powerless [weak, sick], Christ died for the ungodly" (5:6). The righteousness of God has been vindicated in Christ's life and death—an atonement for human sin. Human beings need have no merit at all in order to claim the benefits of Christ's death. For he died for the ungodly, for those who lacked any piety of their own. There is hope for the most needy person spiritually, since it was for such persons that Jesus died: his death was a death to reconcile enemies. And our text indicates that Christ died at just the right time. Humanity had to learn that neither ritual, nor art, nor philosophy, nor law could deliver people from the guilt and power of sin. Only the death of the eternal Son of God could reconcile God and humanity. But Jesus loved us enough to go to the cross for us.

A voluntary death in behalf of others is rare. Only occasionally will one lay down his life for a righteous and a worthy person. But the greatness of the love of God is evident in that Christ died for those who can only be described as sinners, as those who have revolted against God and his holy will.

Full Salvation Through Christ: 5:9-11

We have seen that the New Testament associates our redemption with the blood, death, and cross of Christ. Here redemption is associated with the blood. Through the shedding of his precious blood, we sinners have been reconciled to God. In Christ we have been declared righteous by God, that is "justified." And Christ took on himself the divine punishment of sin as Isaiah writes so beautifully:

> Surely he took up our infirmities
> and carried our sorrows,
> yet we considered him stricken by God,
> smitten by him, and afflicted.
> But he was pierced for our transgressions,
> he was crushed for our iniquities;
> the punishment that brought us peace was upon him,
> and by his wounds we are healed.
> We all, like sheep, have gone astray,
> each of us has turned to his own way;
> and the Lord has laid on him
> the iniquity of us all.
>
> He was oppressed and afflicted,
> yet he did not open his mouth;
> he was led like a lamb to the slaughter,
> and as a sheep before her shearers is silent,
> so he did not open his mouth.
>
> *Isaiah 53:4-7*

This spiritual deliverance by the Lord's suffering servant is connected in the New Testament with the healing ministry of our Lord (Matthew 8:17). Hebrews declares that Christ was sacrificed to take away sin (9:28). Christ bore our sins in his body on the "tree" (cross; see 1 Peter 2:24). In short, Christ died for our sins (1 Corinthians 15:3). And when the Ethiopian treasurer was reading Isaiah 53, Philip began "with that very passage . . . and told him the good news about Jesus" (Acts 8:32-35). Isaiah summarizes the important ministry of the suffering servant by writing simply: "For the transgression of my people he was stricken" (53:8).

Saved by a Living Lord

It is clear that reconciliation with God has come through the sacrifice of our Lord on the cross of Golgotha. But here Paul goes on to state that we shall be saved through [or by] his life. In a sense we may say that half of Paul's theology rested on the vicarious death of our Lord, for Christ died to conquer the forces of sin and death (cf. Hebrews 2:14, 15). The other half of Paul's theology is that Christ arose from the dead: He is alive forevermore! *He lives!* Therefore, as Jesus had entreated his disciples we are to abide in him (John 15:4-7). Paul expands this idea to the full. The Christian is "in Christ." This concept which Paul mentions about 130 times, grows out of his experience with the living Lord. The turning point for this erstwhile persecutor of Christians was the appearance of the living Lord Jesus to the stubborn and misguided Saul as he neared Damascus around AD 35. The knowledge that Jesus of Nazareth was now the living Lord of glory was simply devastating to him. His whole theology had to be revamped. He had to learn that the Messiah was by God destined to suffer and die, and to rise again, and that the historic Jesus of Nazareth was in very truth the Messiah of God.

Paul at once made the surrender of faith, and henceforth he lived under the lordship of Jesus the Messiah; indeed, he lived in conscious fellowship with Christ Jesus through the power of the Holy Spirit. The Christian, for Paul, is reconciled to God through the sacrificial death of Jesus on the cross. He is declared righteous through a faith union with the resurrected and living Christ Jesus. This theology is developed more fully in chapters 6 and 8 of Romans.

Belonging to Adam's Race
or Belonging to Christ's "Race": 5:12-21

Romans 5:12-21 is one of the more obscure passages of the English Bible. Part of our problem is that we have not learned to think like the apostle. Paul saw the historic first man (the Hebrew "Adam" means man) as the source of all human sin. The first man sinned against God by his revolt—by his disobedience to the divine command. The consequence of that sin is that death as we know it came upon all humanity, for humanity has continued in the evil way started by Adam. The Greek here is compact: "Therefore, just as sin entered the world through one man, and death through sin, and in this way death came to all men, because all sinned (5:12). The intention seems to go farther than that Adam set a bad example. Rather, sin and all its consequences (summed up in the word "death") had their beginning, their source, in Adam; thus, all of Adam's race, all humanity, is both sinful and mortal. Paul does not explain the how of this transmission; he simply states the fact of the universality of "depravity" and mortality.

Paul thinks of the law as being like litmus paper which shows up acid in a liquid being tested. The law reveals sin. What then about the human race in the long era before there was a written law? Paul first sets forth the general rule that where there is no law to sin against, sin in the full sense is not committed (5:13); yet the phenomenon which the law calls sin did exist. Sin was there, but it was not fully reckoned to those who sinned. Yet Paul points out that the consequence of sin, namely death, also reigned over all who lived and sinned in the era of unwritten law, the period from Adam to Moses. Paul returns to this thought in 5:20: law was added to make the trespass increase or abound. After the time of Moses, sin was more self-conscious on the part of Israel. Having fuller light concerning the holiness and goodness of God, they more consciously sinned against him.

Now we come to the most difficult problem in this section. In what sense did humanity sin because of the trespass of the first man? One interpretation is that of "immediate imputation," which holds that the entire race was held guilty of the trespass of its first representative, Adam. Another view, called "mediate imputation," sees Adam as the one who infected the race with sin and depravity; each person in turn became guilty of his own sin. In view of later revelation, it is this latter view which appeals to many people today. The law of Moses specified: "Fathers shall not be put to death for their children, nor children put to death for their fathers; each is to die for his own sin" (Deuteronomy 24:16). Good king Amaziah of Judah put to death the assassins who had murdered his father, but he spared their sons "in accordance with what is written in the Book of the Law of Moses where the Lord commanded: 'Fathers shall not be put to death for their children, nor children put to death for their fathers; each is to die for his own sins' " (2 Kings 14:6). Later in Israel there was a proverb:

> The fathers eat sour grapes,
> and the children's teeth
> are set on edge.

But through the prophet Ezekiel the Lord stated: "As surely as I live, declares the Sovereign Lord, you will no longer quote this proverb in Israel. For every living soul belongs to me, the father as well as the son—both alike belong to me. "The soul [person] who sins is the one who will die" (Ezekiel 18:2-4). The entire Bible emphasizes personal accountability to God for one's life. The gospel itself calls for personal responsibility: "Repent and believe the gospel;" that is, turn from sin, and put your trust in God and in the mediator with the Father, Jesus Christ.

Contrast of Christ with Adam

Adam, then, introduced sin and death into the human race; death as we know it is the fruit of sin. Now Paul turns to Christ and emphasizes that the gift which Christ brings is vastly greater than what we have lost through Adam. The opposite of sin is righteousness, and the opposite of death is life. Adam brought sin and death, but Christ brings their opposites: righteousness and life; that is, fullness of life, both here and now and in eternity. Adam's legacy to the race followed his one act of disobedience (called the fall). But Christ's gift of righteousness and life follows many human transgressions. Adam brought the pollution and condemnation of sin, but in his grace Christ brought the righteousness of God and "justification," that is, the state of having divine righteousness as a gift. The language of Romans 5:18 sounds as though both the condemnation through Adam, and the justification through Christ, are parallel and automatic. But are they?

The fact that all human beings are given divine righteousness as a gift has been interpreted three ways: (1) Strict predestinarian theology holds that "all" here means all the elect. A review of the entire New Testament, however, has led many of us to hold that the atonement of Christ was: (a) adequate for all people, (b) offered to all people, and (c) intended for all people. Salvation depends upon each person's response to the gospel invitation, a response which is always made in the enabling power of the Holy Spirit.

(2) The second interpretation of Romans 5:18 is that *all* means that every last human being, no matter how wicked and how impenitent, will *ultimately be saved*. This doctrine is called universalism. In the ancient church, the writer Origen (c.185-c.254) seems to have been somewhat attracted to this view, and the same may be said of the Swiss theologian, Karl Barth (1886-1968). But the Christian church, on the basis of the word of Christ himself, has firmly rejected universalism. Jesus said that the wicked "will go away to eternal punishment, but the righteous to eternal life" (Matthew 25:46).

(3) The third interpretation is that all people are actually sinful, guilty, and lost so long as they reject the Savior; but that all are potentially saved; they are righteous, and in grace, if and only if they turn from sin and make the surrender of faith. Spiritually the case is somewhat similar to the man who had committed a major crime in early nineteenth-century America, in the days when John Marshall was the chief justice of the U.S. Supreme Court. Friends in high places succeeded in having the convicted criminal pardoned by the president of the United States. Strangely enough the criminal said: "I reject the pardon." Then no one seemed to know what to do. The case was referred to the attorney general of the United States, but he stated candidly: "The law is not clear!" Finally the matter was referred

to the Supreme Court, and it was Chief Justice Marshall himself, one of the greatest jurists in the history of the country, who wrote the decision of the high court. "A pardon," said the court, "is a statement which offers a criminal immunity to his crime. If the man rejects the pardon, he shall hang."

Now the New Testament is clear from beginning to end that Christ died for all people. This is said over and over again, and in various ways. God gave his one and only Son that everyone who believes in him might have eternal life (John 3:16). God did not spare his only Son but delivered him up for us all (Romans 8:32). It is our judgment (or conviction) that one died in behalf of everyone (2 Corinthians 5:14). By the grace of God Christ tasted death in behalf of all (Hebrews 2:9).

The New Testament is also fully clear that God longs to see every human being turn to Christ and be saved. He wishes all people to be saved and to come to a [full] knowledge of the truth (2 Timothy 2:4). The Lord is patient with us, for he does not want anyone to perish, but [he wants] all to come to repentance (2 Peter 3:9). Yet believers are by God's foreknowledge called the "elect" (1 Peter 1:2)!

A good illustration of the paradox before us is found in Acts 13. Paul and Barnabas went into the Jewish synagogue in Antioch to witness to the good news of salvation through Christ. As usual, the gospel invitation went out, both to the Jews and the Gentiles. Vast numbers responded and became Christian believers, especially from among the Gentiles. This excited the hostility of some of the Jews, who refused to become believers on Jesus the Messiah; they also opposed the conversion of Gentiles to the Christian faith. Note now the clarity of Paul on the matter of personal accountability. He did not say to the unbelieving Jews: "What a pity! I see that you are not among God's 'elect'." On the contrary, Paul placed the responsibility for their rejection of Jesus solely on themselves. He said, "Since you reject [the good news of Christ] . . . and do not consider yourselves worthy of eternal life, we now turn to the Gentiles" (Acts 13:46). On the other hand, the Gentiles who were present "honored the word of the Lord"; that is they joyfully responded to the good news of salvation through Jesus, the crucified and risen Lord. And then Luke, the author of Acts, adds (concerning these open-hearted Gentiles): "And all who were appointed for eternal life believed" (Acts 13:48).

We must remember, of course, that God is God, and we must not presume to understand fully his will and action. But as nearly as we can formulate the truth of the paradox, it would be something like this: The damnation of men and women is of themselves; it is they who refuse to repent and believe. But the salvation of men and women is of God, for he provided, at great cost, a Savior to die for them. He loved them with an eternal love. From all eternity such penitent believers were precious to him, and in time he called them to repentance and faith in the power of his Spirit.

We should also note one more emphasis in Romans 5: that is the contrast between the solidarity in sin which the human race had in Adam and the solidarity in redemption which Christ has now effected. We are the body of Christ. The apostle is so exultant about the righteousness and life which are now available in Christ that for a moment he seems to ignore the fact that many people—people who are offered full pardon and eternal life through Christ—wickedly refuse to accept the glorious gift of forgiveness and grace. Yet for Paul human faithlessness does not annul the faithfulness of God! "What if some did not have faith? Will their lack nullify God's faithfulness? Not at all!" (Romans 3:3).

5

The Believer Delivered

(Romans 6)

Union with Christ Means Holy Living: 6:1-10

With lots of enthusiasm Paul has argued persuasively that the standing of the Christian believer is perfect. On the basis of his faith, God himself declares the believer to be righteous. This standing is not the result of moral or theological perfection, but comes about solely because the believer has made the surrender of faith. God has poured his love into his heart. He is "in Christ," with all the benefits which flow from that relationship.

Are We Against the Law?

Now Paul suddenly asks if this doctrine was intended to teach that it doesn't matter how we live. Shall we go on sinning so that grace may increase? His response is a vigorous phrase in Greek which is about equivalent to "I should say not!" The King James Version is even stronger: "God forbid." The German may be roughly translated, "That is far [off the track]!" The doctrine that it doesn't matter how Christians live, for they are not obligated to keep the law, is called antinomianism (lawlessness); and Paul opposed this with all his might.

Union with Christ

Greek and English both belong to the Indo-European

family of languages. In these languages it is possible to add a particular meaning to a word by means of a prefix: the prefix *in* means *not,* so not eligible is ineligible; the final letter of the prefix may be modified: not possible is impossible; not resistible is ir-resistible. The Greek prefix *syn* means *with,* or in English compound words, *co-.* Thus when the right combination of instruments sound forth, we have a *symphony: (syn* means co- and *phoneo* in Greek means to sound forth).

Paul uses a number of *co-* words to express the union of the believer with the Savior, the Lord Jesus. His first reply to the thought of antinomianism is: Don't you know that we believers have died to sin? so how can a spiritual corpse sin again? Just as Christ physically died and was buried, so we are *co-buried* with him (one word in Greek). In our baptism, declares the apostle, we were *baptized into Christ,* even into his death. By faith we are *united with him* in our baptism. And since he died, we too shall *die* to sin, for we *live* (have eternal life) in Christ.

Paul continues with his exposition of our union with Christ. Our Lord was literally buried, laid in the tomb. Therefore Paul declares that because of our union with our Savior, we are *co-buried* with him in our baptism; burial is the proof that death is real. And just as Christ was raised from the dead through the glory of the Father, through his glorious might, we too may thus *(houtōs)* walk in newness of life.

New Life in Christ

No corpse can be taught to walk. But those who have "newness of life" through union with the living Christ are enabled by his Spirit to walk in what was called in the first century "the way" (Acts 9:2; 19:9, 23; 22:4; 24:14, 22). And just as we were "united" (another co- word) with him in his death, so will we be "united" with him in his resurrection (new life!). For we know that the "old self" (person, not male) was *co-crucified* with Christ in order that the body of sin might be *rendered powerless.* This word, *rendered powerless,* is used thirty-five times by Paul. It does not mean "destroy," as if, for example, Satan is put out of existence (cf. Hebrews 2:14, 15); rather, in reference to those who are in Christ, Satan has lost the power to enslave them further. They are liberated. Here Paul is insisting that our redemption in Christ has liberated us from the bondage to the "flesh," that sinful nature called by theologians "original sin," which does not mean the fall, but rather the depravity which has come to the race as a result of the fall of Adam. Christ sets men free! In his first Letter to the church at Corinth, Paul writes: "Do you not know that the wicked will not inherit the kingdom of God? Do not be deceived: Neither the sexually immoral nor idolators nor adulterers nor male prostitutes nor homosexual offenders nor thieves nor the greedy nor drunkards nor slanderers nor swindlers will inherit the kingdom of God." A rather formidable word! But Paul goes on to show that the power of Christ sets free by his Spirit those who yield to him in penitence and faith: "And that is what some of you were. But you were washed, you were sanctified [made holy], you were justified [declared righteous] in the name of the Lord Jesus Christ and by the Spirit of our God" (1 Corinthians 6:9-11).

Spiritual Liberation

The consequence of this spiritual liberation in Christ is that we should no longer be slaves to sin. Then Paul adds that after one has died he has been freed from sin (literally has been declared righteous in relation to sin). Sin loses its appeal when one becomes a corpse! Sin now is a matter of revulsion rather than attraction.

If we died with Christ. There are two words for *if* in Greek: the one is used in cases of uncertainty: *If* it is raining in Rome . . . (and I have no idea what the weather is there today); here the Greek word is *e-an,* (This is the word used by Gamaliel in Acts 5:38 when he raised the question: "*If* the message is of men. . . . ") The other Greek *if (ei)* assumes that the *if-clause* is true: If the day where I am today is pleasant and breezy—and it is—here the word is *ei.* (Amazingly this is the word used by Gamaliel in Acts 5:39: "*If* the message is of God, beware lest you even be found

'God-fighters!' ") Here in Romans 6:8 Paul uses the *if* to mean *since:* "Now if [since] we died with Christ, we believe that we will also [co-]live with him." When the finger of God touches the spiritually dead person, he springs to life and really begins to live!

Paul reminds his readers that the risen Christ is now immortal; he cannot die again, for his death was once for all. (Note how this once-for-all quality of his death is stressed in Hebrews: Christ made his sacrifice for our sins "once" [Hebrews 9:28]. He entered into the Most Holy Place "once for all" [Hebrews 9:12]. We have been made holy by the "once for all" sacrifice of the body of Christ: [Hebrews 10:10].) And this risen Christ *lives* his life to God (Romans 6:10). In the days of his flesh, prior to his death on the cross, Christ was human. And by becoming a sacrifice for sin on the cross of Golgotha, he identified fully with human need. But now the risen Lord has been glorified; he doesn't need to look forward any longer to his "baptism" of suffering on the hill outside the holy city. He now lives to God. Perhaps Paul chooses this very phrase to parallel our co-dying with Christ, our being co-buried with him, our being co-vivified with him (made alive spiritually), our being co-raised (ascended) with him, and our being co-seated with him in the heavenly realms. In such a context the statement of fact that Christ lives to God becomes an admonition for believers to imitate: We shall no longer live in sin and look forward to sin's penalty, death; we shall live unto God, seeing that we have made the transition from death to life, to fullness of life!

Claiming Victory by Faith: 6:11-14

In the area of physical life we are not born by our own initiative; likewise, our adolescence simply comes of itself. So does old age. But in spiritual matters these analogies do not hold. Repentance is not automatic; neither is faith in Christ, nor spiritual victory over sin. We claim victory by faith. Hence Paul writes: "count yourselves dead to sin." Luther warns us that the "old man," although "drowned" in baptism, can nevertheless swim quite well! For the Christian the evil propensities in human nature are like a tiger locked up in a cage. If we open the door, the tiger can be quite disruptive! When the Spirit of God nudges believers toward victory, they can either ignore him and sink down in sin, or they can claim newness of life in Christ by faith and walk as children of light. Both the relation of death to sin and the state of being alive to God in Christ Jesus are spiritual realities only if claimed by faith. From start to finish the Christian life is lived by faith. Moment by moment spiritual victory must be appropriated by faith. Every thought must be taken captive and brought to obedience in Christ (2 Corinthians 10:5). Sin would like to reign like a king, but we must not let sin reign; victory in Christ is possible. There is even a sense in which we need not "fight" with temptation. Rather, we should ever be on the alert to recognize sin when it seeks to overcome us. It is not a sin to be tempted. But it is sin to obey the evil desires, those desires which come to us because we remain human even after we have become partakers of the divine nature (2 Peter 1:4).

How Attain Victory

A writer named H. M. Savacool once wrote a tract, "How to Attain Victory in the Christian Life." The five chief suggestions are:

(1) We must make the surrender of faith. This is both a beginning act of total surrender, and a continuing surrender to the Lord as new issues arise. Today we may be fully in the Lord's will, and tomorrow we may be tempted to remain silent when the Lord wants us to speak up for him; or we may be tempted to give less to the Lord's cause than he wishes us to give.

(2) Savacool pleads that Christian disciples may be open to a heightened devotion to the Lord Jesus. This calls for feeding on the Word of God, for seeking to be open to the gentle impulses of God's Spirit, and for prompt obedience to those impulses which come from God. A farmer, for example, may reap a harvest which pays off better than anticipated. The Lord may suggest to him that he give a sizable gift ("unreasonable," cries the flesh) to some program of the church which is running low in

funds. Will he strengthen his devotion to the head of the church, or will he be disobedient?

(3) Be positive. Concentrate on doing the will of God—not on "fighting" what you want to avoid. It is as we obey that we grow more mature in the Christian faith and life. As we obey the impulses of the Spirit, they come to us with ever greater clarity. Each hour, each day, each week God knows exactly what we ought to do, and he will lead us if we "listen."

(4) Victory in Christian living does not mean that we always have smooth sailing. God knows best how to chasten us, how much to allow us to suffer, so that we come forth refined as gold which has been put through the fire (1 Peter 1:6, 7). Job did not understand his many trials, much less did his three theologizing "friends," but God knew what he was doing. In the end God's goodness shone like the sun. It is not a joy to undergo trials, but they are the price of "righteousness and peace" (Hebrews 12:11).

(5) Give a wide berth to what you know to be your weakness. The converted drunkard will avoid social situations in which he may be tempted by the hypnotic odor of alcohol. Likewise all true Christian disciples will avoid unnecessary exposure to what they know to be their weakness.

The phrase, "Do not let" (Romans 6:12), does not sound like a firm prohibition, especially in its usual form: "Do not let sin reign." The problem is that in English we have no third person imperative. But the force of the Greek is clear: See to it that sin does not go on reigning! Do not take a passive, much less a defeatist, attitude! Take whatever steps are necessary to attain victory! That could mean prayer, calling other disciples to prayer, or even fasting. The happy fact is that victory is possible, especially if sin is "nipped in the bud" and not allowed to blossom. The formula for defeat is making allowance for the sin, and putting off working toward overcoming it. What happens is that the lure of the sin gets fearfully strong; finally, the human victim goes down in defeat. By that time he has also rationalized his behavior so that he is able to argue eloquently that his way of life is not wrong.

A Fearful Warning

Jeremy Taylor (1613-1667), was an Anglican scholar, writer, and author of numerous books. He was a minister of the gospel. He was in prison three times because of the unsettled conditions in Great Britain in his days. He finally served as a bishop in Ireland. In a startling manner he has described the downward course of a person who "plays" with sin until he is destroyed by it: "First it startles him, then it becomes pleasing, then delightful, then frequent, then habitual, then confirmed; then the man is impenitent, then obstinate, then resolved never to repent, then damned" (quoted in A. H. Strong, *Systematic Theology,* p. 651).

We must not forget however, the gracious work of God and the role of God's people in restoring the sinning believer to holiness. The stumbling of the backslider may at first not be detected by human eyes, but God knows about it. And God will bring twinges of conscience to the stumbling and wavering believer. He will also bring chastisement into his life. Finally, other Christians will take notice of the one who has strayed from the way and will pray for him, warn him, and beg him to repent and make a clean break with his sin. What the careless believer does about his sin depends upon his response to the witness of God's Word, of God's Spirit, and of God's people. If he resumes Bible reading, prayer, and church attendance, there is good hope that he will repent fully and return to a life of self-denial and holiness. If he clings to his sin, the future will become more and more bleak. Paul knew of the tragic lives of two men, Hymenaeus and Alexander, who had "shipwrecked their faith" (1 Timothy 1:19, 20); later he mentions Hymenaeus and Philetus who "wandered away from the truth" (2 Timothy 2:17, 18). These men surely went against all the efforts of the Lord and of his people to lead them back to a sound faith and life. But sin works like a drug. The deeper one sinks in sin, the more feeble the voice of conscience becomes, the more delightful the sin becomes to the "flesh," and the weaker the witness of the Holy Spirit becomes. For sin carries its own hypodermic needle with which to soothe the miseries of conscience brought on by living in sin.

God Is Faithful

God is not dead, of course. He is faithful, merciful, and he knows how to awaken sinners. Peter could curse and swear, and even deny his Lord. Yet the Lord took such steps that Peter repented with bitter tears; later, the Lord Jesus had a session with him to restore him to spiritual wholeness and commission him to be an apostle. The New Testament literally abounds with both (1) warnings about the necessity to "watch and pray" (Matthew 26:41), and (2) assurances that God is able to keep all believers for a faithful end in Christ. In Ephesians, Paul instructs the believers in detail about the "whole armor" they are to put on so as to achieve the full and final victory of faith (Ephesians 6:10-20). In a number of his letters, Paul is careful to point out that God is able, and that God intends, to keep them from final defeat and apostasy. In his first known letter, Paul appeals to his readers to be "alert and self-controlled" (1 Thessalonians 5:6); he expresses the concern that they may be "blameless at the coming of our Lord Jesus Christ" (1 Thessalonians 5:23). In his second letter to the same church, Paul tells the Christians to "stand firm and hold to the teachings" (2:15) he had given them; but his ultimate confidence was in God's faithfulness: ". . . the Lord is faithful, and he will strengthen and protect you from the evil one" (2 Thessalonians 3:3). In his third letter Paul encourages his readers to "stand firm" in Christian freedom (that is, avoid legalism) (Galatians 5:1). And again he writes: "I am confident in the Lord that you will take no other view" (Galatians 5:10). Paul also had the confidence that his Corinthian readers would be saved, "if [since] you hold firmly to the word" (1 Corinthians 15:2). They are to "stand firm" (1 Corinthians 16:13). But once again Paul has the confidence that God "will keep you strong to the end" (1 Corinthians 1:8). Both themes run throughout the entire New Testament: (1) Cling to Christ and be faithful; and (2) God will enable you to do it!

Offer Yourself to God

In various eras of the history of the church there were antinomian teachers who saw the human body as hopelessly evil, as unredeemable. But the apostles who had been taught of Christ did not hold to that unsound view. There is no such thing as serving God in the inner self, while indulging in sin with the body. Each of us is just one person. It is true that we have the capacity to think, and we call that the mind. We have the capacity for fellowship with God, and we call that the spirit. We have the capacity to relate to this earth, including other beings, and we call that the body. In Paul's world a person as a being comprised of several senses (such as sight and smell) could be called a soul. (Today, however, we use the term soul for the inner self which survives the death of the body; as the hymn says, we have a never-dying soul to save.) In the New Testament, the word soul can be converted into an adjective, so that people who live for the pleasures of the senses are called natural or sensual (1 Corinthians 2:14; 15:44, 46; James 3:15; Jude 19).

Now God does not wish us to be dominated by the pleasures of the senses so that we are *sensual* ("soulish" in the New Testament). God desires that we bring our very bodies under the control of the Holy Spirit. In Paul's way of speaking we are then "spiritual" (1 Corinthians 2:15; 14:37; Galatians 6:1), and we constitute a "spiritual house" (1 Peter 2:5). The Holy Spirit gives us "spiritual gifts" (Romans 1:11; 1 Corinthians 12:1). These gifts of the Spirit can be literally called "spirituals," that is, "spiritual gifts," the several gifts which the Holy Spirit confers on us (1 Corinthians 12:1; 14:1).

If a person has therefore not made the surrender of faith to Christ, he is still a natural person. But if he is "filled with the Spirit," a theme found much in the Acts and in the epistles of the New Testament, he is *spiritual* and his very body is then used in the service of God. The members of the body can be used to serve sin (hands can commit murder) or they can be instruments used in the service of God (hands can distribute gifts of food or even God's Word); tongues can swear or they can proclaim the gospel to those who have not yet passed from darkness into light. "For sin shall not be your master" (literally, shall not lord it over you) Romans 6:14. The Christian is no longer to be fleshly or carnal (dominated by evil desires). But the sinner who refrains from a given sinful indulgence because he is still under law has not really crossed from death to life, from the bondage of sin to the glorious liberty of the children of God. Those who are under grace, who are in Christ, long to please God in thought, word, and deed.

Contrasts and Challenges: 6:15-23

Contrast No. 1: Under Law or Under Grace

Paul now raises a very human question. Since we are not under law, but under God's grace, shall we (or may we) then sin? Again we have that brief Greek expression which is about like "I should say not!" At this point Paul mentions a new consideration. He does not back up an inch from his basic contention that Christians are under grace: "Blessed is the man whose sin the Lord does not count against him" (Psalm 32:2; Romans 4:8). The new consideration is: We indicate who our master is by the one we obey! We are either *slaves to sin*—and sin leads to death and ultimately to that eternal separation from God which is death indeed; or we are "love slaves" of God, in *obedience* to him because we love him; and those who love God have the gift of *righteousness* through Christ.

Contrast No. 2: Slaves of Sin or Enslaved to Righteousness

Thanks be to God, cries Paul, that you are now liberated or set free from sin and its slavery. This liberation took place when you responded to the gospel, with its call for repentance and surrender, by becoming obedient to the gospel call. The Greek indicates that these Roman converts *obeyed from the heart* [*wholeheartedly obeyed;* NIV] the teaching or doctrine of those who proclaimed the good news.

Intensify Your Loving Obedience!

Because of the weakness of your "flesh," says Paul, allow me to "put this in human terms. . . . Just as you used to offer the

parts of your body in slavery to impurity and to ever-increasing
wickedness, so now offer them in slavery to righteousness leading
to holiness." There is no such thing as imputed righteousness
apart from simultaneous imparted righteousness. Imputed
righteousness is perfect righteousness, while imparted righteousness is not fully realized because of human weakness; hence,
there is a continual need for the grace of God. But, Paul implies,
growth in Christian character is both possible and desirable.

Looking back, Paul reminds them that in their pre-conver-
sion days, when they were slaves to sin, they were utterly devoid
of the control of righteousness. Paul holds up the mirror of
God's holy law so that the Roman believers can once more see
what they looked like spiritually when they lived in the shame of
sin! Without naming a single sin, Paul comments briefly that
slavery to sin leads to eternal *death* (separation from God
eternally). Once more the apostle goes over the theme of redemption: "Now that you have been set free from sin and have become [love] slaves to God, the benefit you reap leads to holiness,
and the result is eternal life" (literally, you have your fruit unto
sanctification, and the end [is] eternal life).

Finally, with a grand flourish, Paul cries: "For the wages
[earned!] of sin is death, but the [free] gift of God is eternal life in
Christ Jesus our Lord. Salvation is a free gift; we take of the
water of life *gratis* (Revelation 22:17). In prophecy Isaiah sang:

> Come, all you who are thirsty,
> come to the waters;
> and you who have no money,
> come, buy and eat!. . .

6

Liberation, Not Perfectionism

(Romans 7)

United to the Law or United with
Christ Through Faith: 7:1-6

Paul now lovingly addresses his Jewish brothers and sisters, reminding them that the law is binding only for so long as they are alive. If a person passes away, he or she is no longer subject to law. By way of illustration Paul turns to the marriage bond. A woman is bound to her husband as long as he lives. But should the husband die, the woman is set free from the marriage contract. Therefore, as long as the husband is living she has no right to give herself to another man; that would make her an adulteress. The Greek reads literally: "Therefore while the husband is living she will be called an adulteress if she *'be'* to another man" (7:3). Luther's German version reads literally: "Where she *is with* another man, since the husband lives, she will be called an adulteress." The verb used of the wife's unfaithfulness is the subjunctive form of the verb *to be:* "If she be" is therefore equivalent to, "If she give herself [to anyone other than her legal husband]." The translation, "give herself," is the best we can offer in English—and is used by Karl Barth in his commentary on Romans.

76

Death Sets Free

Now we come to a wholly new situation. What if the woman's husband should die? The answer is that the law requiring her to be faithful to her spouse no longer has any hold on her. She has no spouse. Her husband has died. The law of marriage itself still stands, but it does not apply to her, for she is now a widow, not a married woman. In that case, says Paul, she will not be called an adulteress if she were to marry a second husband. Death has intervened and released her from the authority of the law.

The Spiritual Application

At this point Paul sets forth what he has been aiming at: Christ's death on the cross has inaugurated the new covenant. His shed blood accomplished our redemption. The new covenant is not one of slavery to law, but one of liberation! When people enter this covenant, divine power is granted to them to live by love. God, in fact, pours his love into their hearts so that they obey God because they love him, not in submission to a legal code. Such liberation is commonly called, "Christian freedom." This is freedom to walk in holiness and love, not freedom to break the law of God.

In Union with Christ Through Faith

As members of the new covenant which Jesus established by his sacrifice on the cross, we are now "married" to another spouse: we are in a faith-union with the Son of God. Instead of naming our Lord, Paul describes him as the one *who was raised from the dead,* (7:4) a clear reference to the resurrection on Easter morning. When people surrender in faith to the crucified Son of God, the same power which raised Christ from the dead is available to them "in order that [they] ... might bear fruit to God. For when we were controlled by the sinful nature (that is, as long as we lived according to *the flesh,* in disregard of God and his holy will), the *sinful passions were at work in our bodies* (Greek: "in our members"), so that we bore fruit for [or to] *death*

(7:4-5). In other words, it is "natural" for an unregenerated person to live in sin. And it even seems to aggravate the impulses of the "flesh" to be told not to follow the flesh and its drives! The sinner who knows only the law, that is, what he ought to do, and whose heart has not been melted by the love of God in the power of the Holy Spirit, becomes even more defiant of God and his will: "the sinful passions [are] aroused by the law." Law cannot save sinners.

In the immediate context, one can see only a bad outcome of being confronted with the law of God. Law in itself has no power to change the "heart," the inner self of the sinner; indeed, law makes everything worse spiritually for the unregenerated.

Yet Law Can Serve a Good Purpose

Elsewhere we learn, however, that the very confrontation of the unconverted person with the holy law of God can do more than drive the sinner to be even more defiant; it can also drive the sinner to such distress and despair that in desperation he flees to the Savior! Paul compared the good function of the law in relation to the unconverted person to that of a child attendant. The task of the attendant, usually a slave, was to take a child "to and from school and to superintend his conduct generally" (Arndt-Gingrich. *Greek-English Lexicon,* p. 608). (The word did not mean a schoolteacher. See Galatians 3:19-23, also the discussion in Romans 7:7-14.)

Death Releases

Finally, Paul says that when we are converted, we Christians really "die" to legalism: "by dying to what once bound us, we have been released from the law" (7:6). The way of law and the way of love are altogether different paths; the first leads to pride and self-righteousness, if one is sufficiently blind; and it leads to despair, if one is honest. (See the unusually fine essay by Michael Sattler (d. 1527), "On Two Kinds of Obedience," that of law and that of love, in *The Legacy of Michael Sattler,* translated and edited by John H. Yoder, pp. 121-125.)

The Spirit Enables

At this point Paul mentions a theme which he will develop in chapter 8: "we serve in the new way [Greek, "newness"] of the Spirit, and not in the old way ["oldness"] of the written code" (7:6). Legalism is concerned with the letter of the law, which one has an obligation to obey whether the obedience is a pleasure or a burden! But the Spirit-filled disciple finds the Christian life and Christian service a joyful delight. He loves the one whose will he does!

The illustration Paul uses here is moving and powerful. The people of God were first "married" to law (legalism), and that was a tragic union; it did not produce spiritual fruit, for human nature is such that legalism is not capable of bearing fruit pleasing to God. By his sacrifice on the cross, Christ did away with law as the means of justification. But now that God's people are justified in a faith-union with Christ, they are able, in the power of his Spirit, to bear fruit of "love, joy, peace, patience, kindness, goodness, faithfulness, gentleness, and self-control" (Galatians 5:22, 23).

Victory, but Not Perfectionism: 7:7-25

Law Reveals the Evil of the Flesh

Paul realizes what the natural conclusion is, a conclusion which may be logical but which is all wrong: The law is sin! "Absolutely not," cries the apostle; as a matter of fact, the law performs a wholesome function! It is God's law which forces a person to acknowledge that he has a human nature which is self-willed and selfish. Paul declares that he would not have recognized his sinful nature if the law had not "kept saying" [this is force of the Greek tense; A. T. Robertson, *Grammar*, 882f.] "You shall not have evil desire" (7:7). Both the Froschauer and the Luther versions use the word *lust* for that which the law discovered, forbade, and aggravated in Paul. The Greek word is actually used of both good and evil desires, cravings, and longings, but here it is obviously used of evil cravings. The words covet and covetousness are a bit more narrow than the Greek (to covet is to long for what someone has), while the English word *lust* points too much to illicit sexual desire. The Greek word is broad, simply pointing here to that which is not allowed by the law of God. Thus, the law kept insisting: "You shall not harbor evil desire," but the sheer prohibition made Paul's inner struggle even more intense. The fact is that in his human nature Paul's determination to have what God's law forbade him became even more intense through his human frustration. (Human nature in its selfish and sinful aspect is called the "flesh" in the New Testament.)

Only the crucified, risen, and enthroned Christ is able by his Spirit to transform a sinner into a *saint,* that is, one who is a partaker of the divine nature. And Paul devotes chapter 8 to this glorious truth. But he is not yet finished describing human cravings—even in the regenerated! Indeed Paul elsewhere describes the continuing battle between the "flesh" and the Spirit of God: he calls it a *conflict*—flesh and Spirit oppose one another when one is tempted. Galatians 5:16-18 describes the rival powers which each seeks to influence the other. (The same Greek word is translated *desire* in Galatians 5:16 and *covet* in Romans 7:7. The Greek word for *evil desire* in both places is really collective in force referring to the *[evil] desires* of the "flesh." The King James Version uses "lust" in both Romans 7 and Galatians 5, but also uses three different English words [*lust, covet,* and *concupiscence*] for the same Greek word!)

Degrees of Sin

Paul closes Romans 7:8 by remarking that "apart from law, sin is dead." That is, if a human being did not have some knowledge of divine law in his conscience, he would not even know what sin is. But as early as Romans 1:18-25, Paul looked at those who had not possessed the written law of God, and he found the so-called heathen both impious and unrighteous (1:18). For they revolted against even the dim light of conscience which emanates from God's beautiful creation. That light is indeed real (Psalm

19), but it is dim for two reasons: (1) God's curse on creation, which will be removed at Christ's glorious return (Romans 8:19-21), and (2) the "noetic" effect of sin—the way it blinds the mind to God's glory displayed in the heavens and on earth. "Their foolish [undiscerning] hearts were darkened" (1:21). Therefore, we have two truths here: (1) Where there is total darkness, there is no sin; and (2) where there is partial darkness, sin is less than a deliberate revolt against God, for guilt is commensurate with light. At this point we recall the greater guilt of the Jews (Romans 2), for they had the fuller and clearer (written) law of God. And the Jews who knew the messianic promises, and had seen the mighty hand of God work miracles through the Messiah, had a greater guilt than the Gentile procurator of Judea, Pontius Pilate, who had ruled only about four years when our Lord stood before him for judgment.

Childhood's Innocence

In Romans 7:9 Paul makes an enigmatic statement. It is translated (NIV): "Once I was alive apart from law," which could refer to the time when he was an innocent child with no guilt before God. If so, this provides genuine support for the oft-repeated statement of Menno Simons that infants and children are in the kingdom of God, and should therefore be seen as "in the church." The passage could also be rendered, "Apart from law I used to live formerly." Ultimately, however, there is no difference in meaning, for this more literal rendering surely relates to the topic before us: having or not having eternal life. In a childish simplicity Paul probably had the same exposure to the holy Word of God as did Timothy, who from his childhood (see Arndt-Gingrich, *Lexicon,* 147) had "known the holy Scriptures, which are able to make [one] . . . wise for salvation through faith in Christ Jesus" (2 Timothy 3:15).

A bit of common sense will help us understand this verse. Paul is not asserting, of course, that as an infant (the word can so be translated) Timothy had understood God's plan of salvation through Christ. Rather, he is reminding Timothy that from his

earliest memory he had been exposed to the Scriptures, and those
Scriptures do set forth the plan of salvation. Paul was un-
doubtedly taught the Scriptures by his devout, Aramaic-speaking
parents (Philippians 3:5). And he speaks of his obedient manner
of life "from my youth," that is, "from the beginning of my life"
(Acts 26:4). Nevertheless we all know that Saul, as an infant, did
not know anything of the sacred Scriptures, nor of the way of life
God desires, nor of God's holy Law, nor of the Messianic salvation which he later discovered to be in Jesus. But in a reasonable
sense he began to learn to walk in the path of an obedient Jewish
child as soon as he had any understanding. As an innocent child
he lived "apart from law"—and at that time he did *live,* he did
have *life,* even eternal life.

The Fall Repeated

But like all other children of Adam, the day came when
Paul deliberately followed his "flesh," rather than the holy Law
of God. Spiritually speaking, he put forth his hand and deliberately "took the forbidden fruit," to use Pilgram Marpeck's
(d. 1556) figure. Later, Paul looked back and saw that he himself
had joined the rest of humanity in being a sinner. It happened
when he faced God's holy command and dared to say, "No! I
will not obey." Paul puts it dramatically: "Sin sprang to life and I
died" (7:9). In the Greek the *I* is emphatic.

Sin Deceives Its Victims

Paul is not blaming God for his disobedience and his con-
sequent experience of beginning to live in defiance of God's law.
God intended that people should enter into a rich life by obeying
his instructions, and by heeding his warnings. "The very commandment that was intended to bring life actually brought
death" (7:10). The fault lay not in the law of God, but in the
stubbornness of human nature, what the New Testament calls
the "flesh." The most telling phrase is the confession, "Sin . . .
deceived me" (7:11). No one starts out to be a drunkard, or a
swindler, or any other shameful sinner. But sin first presents itself

to the individual as being attractive. The person then rationalizes it: "True, it is a slight violation of the known will of God, but there are extenuating circumstances! Surely, it is not too bad if I do it just once!" But having done it once, it is harder to say no the second time, and so the evil may soon become a way of life, and the sinner gets more and more enslaved.

One time in a certain community lived a respected professional. He had sincerely become a Christian and church member. His wife testified that he was a spiritual Christian for their first fifteen years. The couple had a number of children. But one day another married woman began to attract the doctor. He was certain that he would never allow the attraction to get him down. But little by little he went farther and farther. The woman eventually divorced her husband. Somewhere along the line both the man and his wife appealed for help. But by that time he was really on the hook. "I do not have the strength to break with her," he cried. A Christian psychiatrist remarked that that could be true. "Yes," he said, "it may be true now, but there was a time when he could have broken free." Incidentally, the professional finally divorced his loving wife and married the woman who had likewise been deceived. But the second marriage did not last long. Sin slowly but surely broke up three homes and ruined the happiness of all involved—not to mention the way the children were hurt. From having been a conscientious Christian disciple, the man slowly followed the deceptiveness of sin until he finally became so hard that he could even boast of the dozens of pastors who had tried to help him!

Sin Debases; Christ Liberates

There is an ancient Hindu fable of a man who was so "spiritual" that he drank no water; he just licked the grass! Then he went into the army for some years, and when he came home he no longer licked the grass; he was a slave to strong drink! Sin deceives: it offers forbidden pleasures, but brings death. The holy will of God revealed in his commandments and warnings leads to a happy and fulfilled life if obeyed from a heart of love. Our Lord himself told an inquirer: "If you want to enter life, obey the commandments" (Matthew 19:17). It is wise to follow the counsel of the apostle Peter: "Repent, then, and turn to God, so that your sins may be wiped out . . ." (Acts 3:19). Sin leads to slavery and death. Repentance and faith lead to forgiveness, liberation, and life eternal.

Sin Known by Its Fruit

Paul adds that when sin brought on death it was then recognized as sin (7:13). A conscience which is not taught and informed by the Word of God may be a poor guide. How often sinners boast that they can do this or that sin without any compunctions of conscience. But they may have sinned so long that the protests of conscience can no longer be heard! And that is truly a desperate situation. When the misery of sin's slavery becomes evident, then such slaves perceive that sin has become utterly (exceedingly or excessively) sinful. The defeated doctor one time said, "I never thought I would get into this situation!" Romans 7 addresses all believers, warning: Do not allow sin to deceive you! Do not trust the flesh! Nip sin in the bud; do not imagine that you can play with sin without getting caught in its trap!

As a young man I took some younger siblings to the Philadelphia Zoo. One of the places we visited was the lion house. It happened to be feeding time. An employee walked down the boardwalk between cages. The cages were set back far enough that the lions could not reach out to the walk. One lion crouched in the far corner of his cage until the keeper had walked by, then sprang at the man, only to crash against the bars of his huge cage. Had the keeper been careless and overconfident, he could have unlocked the cage and released the lion, only to be overcome. When believers play with sin they are letting sin begin to enslave and destroy them. Isn't it strange how the same sins overcome and kill people in one generation after another? People are overcome because sin carries its own hypodermic, and deceives them.

The "Flesh" Is Not the Human Body

Some of the ancient philosophers are said to have been ashamed that they had a body. That idea is completely anti-Christian. Because of the incarnation the eternal Son of God also had a body, a body just as real as ours. Paul doesn't equate flesh with the body. Rather, it is a force which influences a person to use one's body for sinful purposes. People can either use their bodies (Paul would say their "members") as instruments of righteousness or as instruments of sin. The devil got Judas Iscariot to scheme how to make money out of his position as one of the Twelve. Finally Judas went to the Jewish leaders and came away with his hands full of silver. In contrast, the other apostles used their relationship with Jesus to go to the ends of the earth in the great task of meeting total human need: physical and spiritual. Judas used his hands to receive blood money.

Apart from Christ, Paul confesses that he is "sold as a slave to sin" (7:14). Neither law, nor good works, nor ceremony can redeem and set free a person who is in slavery to the "flesh" and to sin. Walking according to the flesh involves constant frustration: doing what one does not intend, and failing to do what one wishes to do. Paul's own conscience attested to the goodness of the law of God, yet he confessed that he was not able to keep the law—for "I know that nothing good lives in me, that is, in my sinful nature" (Greek: in my flesh, 7:18). Paul does not blame his frustration or weakness on having a body. Rather, it is sin which dwells in him, in his flesh. This sin keeps him from perfectionism; he fails to do the full will of God which he would like to do. "For in my inner being I delight in God's law" (7:22). This is the testimony of a regenerated person. And yet the apostle says that he is conscious of painful failure because of the sinful inclination he has to contend with. "What a wretched man I am!" (7:24). This is not the cry of an unregenerate sinner: such a person thinks he is pretty good!

As far as his mind and intentions are concerned, Paul does not waver; he is a love slave to God: he longs to please him. But as far as the flesh is concerned, he is encompassed with infirmity. In thought, word, and deed he is aware of his need of the grace of God.

At the age of 63, John Wesley (1703-1791), the founder of the evangelical revival in Great Britain, wrote this to a newspaper: "I have told all the world that I am not perfect. . . . I tell you flat, I have not attained the character I draw." This is the testimony of one of the most devout disciples of Christ. Christ's disciples are never able to take pride in their own holiness. On the contrary, they must confess that their only hope is in the grace of God.

The Way of Victory

Victory does not lie in perfection of character or in holiness. It is rather a walking each hour of each day in love, holiness, and obedience—not in the arm of the flesh (self-effort), but in trust in Jesus. It is in a faith-union with him that effectiveness of witness and service is achieved, and perseverance is realized. "Who will rescue me from this body of death? Thanks be to God—through Jesus Christ our Lord!" (7:24-25). This is the theme of Romans 8.

7

The Spirit-Filled Life

(Romans 8)

The Two Minds: 8:1-11

The topic which Paul plans to take up in this section of the Roman letter is a commentary of sorts on Proverbs 23:7: "For as a [man] . . . thinketh in his heart, so is he" (KJV). But Romans 8 is infinitely deeper than any insight which may legitimately be drawn from Proverbs 23. For one thing, the word "thinketh" in Proverbs 23 has the meaning of "putting an evaluation on" something (Brown, Driver, Briggs, p. 1045). Paul is speaking however of putting the mind on something really weighty; he is examining the basic purpose of one's life.

Our Perfect Standing

First of all Paul reviews once more the enormous significance of being declared righteous on the basis of having put one's trust in Christ, and therefore being "in him." We are all children of fallen Adam; in our flesh no good thing dwells; our performance falls short of our intention; but in spite of this, in God's sight we believers are under no divine condemnation at all! God knows that in our hearts we delight in the law of God (Romans 7:22). And the apostle assures us over and over that we have a perfect standing with the Father because of his grace, not by our

87

supposed perfection of life. The great Protestant commentator, Franz Delitzsch (1813-1890), wrote: "Every Christian is compelled to confirm what the Apostle here [Romans 7] says, from his own personal experience. And well for him if he can also confirm the fact that God's law, and therefore God's will, is his delight—that he desires the good, and hates the evil; and indeed in such a way that the sin to which, against his will, he is hurried away, is foreign to his inmost nature" (cited by Lange, 246). Those who are in Christ can indeed testify that in spite of their stumblings and shortcomings, they really do desire to please God; they do love him and they do delight in his holy law. Paul adds a beautiful description of Christians in Romans 8:4: they do not live according to the [their] sinful nature [flesh] but according to the Spirit. A zealous scribe added this descriptive phrase to Romans 8:1 as a safeguard against careless living on the part of the regenerated. But the oldest copies of the Greek New Testament do not include this phrase in verse 1.) It is a major part of the gospel, that all believers—young and old, mature and immature—have a perfect standing with the Father.

Paul's Own Example

If there was ever a man who was tremendously effective as a witness to Christ and his gospel, it was the apostle Paul. Yet he too was human; like Israel's high priests, he was "subject to weakness" (Hebrews 5:2).Thus when Paul stood before the Jewish Sanhedrin, he was no doubt somewhat tense. He was therefore irritated when the presiding high priest, a man named Ananias, told those near Paul to strike him on the mouth. At that point Paul exclaimed with some feeling, "God will strike you, you whitewashed wall! You sit there to judge me according to the law, yet you yourself violate the law by commanding that I be struck!" Then, realizing that some in the Sanhedrin were Pharisees (as he was), and some were their vigorous opponents (Sadducees), Paul boldly identified his cause as a good one, holding to the resurrection of the dead! (Acts 23:1-8). This statement gained him the support he counted on, but he later questioned whether he should have said it (Acts 24:21).

In contrast with Paul, our Lord remained silent when unjust accusations were literally heaped on him—a silence which amazed Pontius Pilate who was presiding at his trial (Mark 15:1-5). It is not difficult to choose between Jesus and Paul as to which gave the "louder" testimony to the enabling grace of God. But yet it should also be noted how tenderly God spoke words of assurance and hope to Paul the night after he stood before the Sanhedrin (Acts 23:11). Although Paul's performance demonstrated his human weakness, God looked at his heart and saw there a deep desire to know Christ and to make him known.

Dr. Kenneth Geiger, in his presidential address to the National Holiness Association's ninety-third annual convention, put it well: "We can today be made perfect in every good work, regardless of the nature of the work or the place to which God has called us. Our obedience can be so full, and our consecration so complete, that at all times we may be found doing the will of God. God knows our potential for service, recognizes the obedience of faith, and looks past imperfect performance to the heart made perfect in love and pure motives."

The Holy Spirit Sets Us Free

Paul indicates that "through Christ Jesus the law of the Spirit of life set me free from the law of sin and death" (8:2). In Christ a new principle is in operation. In conversion there is both a human and a divine action. The human side is to repent and make a decisive break with sin, and to come in brokenness to Christ to make the surrender of faith. On the side of God, it is his Spirit who enables us to see "the exceeding sinfulness of sin," to turn from it, and to make a total surrender to Christ as both Savior and Lord. Those who allow the Spirit to bring them to the decision of the prodigal, "I will arise, and go to my Father," are then incorporated into Christ in an action which the New Testament calls "adoption." Thereafter we do not belong to sin and Satan but to God; human though we are, and still beset with human infirmities, we now have our faces set toward the eternal

city, like Abraham of old. In his almighy power God breaks the
shackles of selfishness and sin, and sets us free! Delitsch was
therefore not satisfied if the believer was aware only of the delight
he found in the law of God and of the depravity of his flesh. He
craved to hear also his testimony "that the spirit of the new life,
having its source in Christ Jesus, has freed him from the urgency
of sin and the condition of death, which were not abrogated
through the law, but only brought to light; so that his will, which
although powerless, was by the law inclined toward what is good,
is now actually capable of good, and opposed to the death still
working in him, as a predominating, overmastering power of life,
to be finally triumphant in glory" (Lange on *Romans,* p. 246).
When we see that God's Spirit can enable those in Christ to
actually please God, we are beginning to get into the truth of
Romans 8.

God Accomplished What Law Could Not Do

"For what the law was powerless to do in that it was
weakened by the sinful nature [flesh], God did . . . " (8:3). This
means that the redemption of humanity has now taken place. We
have more than law to help us. Indeed law could not provide the
strength needed to overcome sin and the flesh. But in his amazing
love and wisdom God sent "his own Son in the likeness of sinful
man." All humanity was totally of the flesh; that is, all people
were by nature corrupted by sin. (The NIV reads "sinful man"
for the Greek "flesh of sin.") Christ identified with us in our
weak humanity and finally died as a sin offering for us. When the
New Testament speaks of Christ "becoming sin," for our sake it
is really pointing to his meek crucifixion as the "Lamb of God"
in our behalf (see 2 Corinthians 5:17-21). He took on our load of
sin by dying as a sin offering in our place. His death was substitu-
tionary or vicarious. But it was more than that; it enabled the
redeemed to walk in love and holiness. We also believe in the victory view of the atonement!

In the context before us, because Paul thinks of the bondage
of all Adam's descendants in sin, he speaks of humanity as flesh.

God "condemned sin in sinful man," the entire race, "in order that the righteous requirements of the law might be fully met in us" (8:3-4)—those not walking according to the flesh (the way people live who do not know God) but who walk "according to the Spirit." The fruit of the Spirit (love, joy, peace, etc., Galatians 5:22, 23) abounds in their lives, and they exercise faithfully the gifts which the Spirit has bestowed upon them. Not least among his blessings is the divine enablement which the Spirit grants to those like Paul who suffer for Christ's sake: even in imprisonment, floggings, lashings, stonings, and shipwrecks.

The Mind of the Flesh

The flesh is human nature at its worst! It is self-centered, self-willed, touchy, proud, concerned with creaturely comfort, pleasure-loving, longing for recognition and praise, delighting in that which is carnal. It resists the holy will and law of God. Paul lists the works of the flesh as "sexual immorality, impurity and debauchery; idolatry and witchcraft; hatred, discord, jealousy, fits of rage, selfish ambition, dissensions, factions and envy; drunkenness, orgies, and the like." Then he adds: "I warn you, as I did before, that those who live like this will not inherit the kingdom of God" (Galatians 5:19-21). He makes a similar list in another letter. He writes: "Do you not know that the wicked will not inherit the kingdom of God? Do not be deceived: Neither the sexually immoral nor idolaters nor adulterers nor male prostitutes nor homosexual offenders nor thieves nor the greedy nor drunkards nor slanderers nor swindlers will inherit the kingdom of God. And that is what some of you were" (1 Corinthians 6:9-11). But at that point a glorious sunburst of divine love and redemption flashes as the apostle adds: "But you were washed, you were sanctified [made holy], you were justified [declared to be righteous] in the name of the Lord Jesus Christ and by the Spirit of our God" (1 Corinthians 6:11).

What Romans 8 asserts is that those who are not born again "put their minds on" or "have their minds set on what that nature [the flesh] desires" (8:5). The evidence that they do not

belong to the Lord is their devotion to a fleshly (carnal) manner
of life. The attitude of the flesh is: "Nobody is going to give me
orders as to what I can or cannot do." The life is a mirror of the
spiritual state. Those who thus put their minds on the things of
the flesh are headed for *death,* and the essential idea of death is
separation from God. When life ceases in a physical body, we say
that the person has entered into death. When a person chooses to
reject God's offer of salvation and holiness, that person enters
into spiritual death: he separates himself from the life which
comes from God. And in the life to come those who have died
outside of Christ and his salvation enter into eternal death, into
an existence apart from the bliss of fellowship with our God and
with his Christ.

Paul declares that "the sinful mind is hostile to God." It does
not submit to God's law (8:7). Paul even asserts that the carnal
mind is not capable of being subject to the law of God! The consequence is that "those controlled by the sinful nature [in the
flesh] cannot please God" (8:8). Finally he states sternly that if
people *live according to the sinful nature,* [they] . . . will die (8:13).
Luther rendered it, "You must die." Death here is spiritual in
character: the certain destiny of those who allow the flesh to control how they live is to be cut off from God. The Greek could be
rendered, "You are about to die": imminence stands for
certainty. J. C. C. von Hofmann (1810-1877) once remarked that,
"The natural man imagines that he owes it to his flesh to satisfy
it" (Godet, 308). This idea is common in our culture today—in
magazines, books, novels, television, the stage. The hunger of the
flesh for satisfaction is insatiable! Yet Paul warns of imminent
death!

The Mind of the Spirit

The happy alternative to this bleak possibility is that when
people are in Christ, they are able by the Holy Spirit's strength to
put their minds on the things of the Spirit: they seek to lead
people to the Savior, they seek to build them up in the faith, and
they seek to help people with every need they have. In other

words, they live according to the love which God pours into their hearts (5:5). Those who have the mind of the Spirit, who are controlled by the Spirit of God (8:9), find life and peace. Life here is eternal life, and peace is total well-being.

In the midst of this important treatise on the necessity of a holy life, Paul suddenly inserts a key idea. He has just assured his recipients that the Spirit of God was dwelling in them. The word *if* ("If the Spirit of God lives in you") means *if indeed, if after all,* or *since* (Arndt-Gingrich, p. 219). Paul is quietly assuring his readers that he has the confidence that they are indeed being transformed by the indwelling Spirit of God. Then he announces that "if anyone does not have the Spirit of Christ, he does not belong to Christ" (8:9). There is no such thing as being a child of God through merely human resources. But there surely is such a thing as living below one's possibilities in Christ, of not being filled with the Spirit; that is, of not being fully yielded and obedient to him.

Claim Your Privileges by Faith: 8:12-17

God Makes Us Holy

Paul states as a fact what is actually a possibility: As to sin, the deeds of *the body* (used here interchangeably with the flesh) are put to death by the Spirit; as to righteousness, *the Spirit* gives *life.* Earlier in the letter Paul had urged them to consider themselves "dead to sin" but "alive to God" through Christ (6:11). This is another way of saying the same thing. By faith we claim eternal life, and holiness of heart.

God Leads Us

Paul suggests another truth we can claim by faith: God leads those who are his children (Paul uses the term *sons* because in the Jewish families of that day a son had the highest possible standing). And he writes the unexpected. One would have expected him to write: Those who are children of God may expect God to lead them. Instead he says: "Those who are led by the Spirit of God are sons of God" (8:14). God opens and closes doors, he puts convictions in our hearts, he gives us general counsel through his Word, and he gives us specific affirmations or warnings through faithful fellow-believers. Read the book of Acts for illustrations: for example: Acts 16:6-10.

God Gives Us an Awareness of Sonship

God does not give us a spirit of fear, like that of a slave. Rather God gives to all believers the standing of Hebrew sons, what Paul calls the "spirit of sonship," what the King James Version calls, "the spirit of adoption."

As children of God read the Word with its many promises, the Holy Spirit puts the assurance in their hearts that the promises apply to them. The Spirit uses the Word to strengthen the faith of those who are "in Christ." The Spirit enables believers, no matter how weak in themselves, to accept the glorious fact that through grace they are "God's children" (8:16), and therefore also "heirs of God and co-heirs with Christ" (8:17). We are heirs of that kingdom which God "promised [to] those who love him" (James 2:5).

The next phrase is transitional: now we *suffer;* then we shall share in his [Christ's] glory.

Present Suffering and Future Glory: 8:18-39

Creation Groans

In a rather mysterious statement in Romans 8:11 Paul had said that through the Spirit God "will ... give life (quicken) to your mortal bodies." Paul connects the miraculous resurrection of our Lord with our own future resurrection from the grave. We now dwell in a mortal body, one subject to disease and death. Indeed, in 1 Corinthians 15 Paul makes a long list of the characteristics of the present body contrasted with the one to be raised up: perishable versus imperishable, dishonor versus glory, weakness versus power, natural versus spiritual (adapted to the glory world), dust of the earth versus from heaven, likeness of Adam versus likeness of Christ, flesh and blood versus "changed," and mortal versus immortal.

The question may well be asked: Does not the Holy Spirit impart a life-enhancing quality to the present mortal body of God's child? In the sense of granting exceptional strength, vigor, divine enablement yes! Paul could be left for dead after being stoned, only to get up, perhaps brush off his clothes, and return to the city (Acts 14:19, 20)! But Paul still had a mortal body, subject to illness (Galatians 4:13). He too looked forward to his quickening. Meanwhile, "our present sufferings are not worth comparing with the glory that will be revealed in us" (8:18). When our Lord returns, when the dead in Christ are raised up, and when those of us who are still alive are changed into the same glorious form as that of our Lord, then we will look back to our trivial sufferings and declare that they were as nothing! This is true of weakness or illness of body, poverty, and temptations.

In 8:19 Paul personifies nature and speaks of it as though it too were longing, waiting "in eager expectation" for Christ's return in glory when he will bring with him those who have died in faith (see 1 Thessalonians 4:13—5:4). Here Paul calls this event the "revelation" of the sons of God: all his children have the high status of sonship! (In 8:19-22 Paul uses a Greek word four times which could be translated as either creation or creature, but it is best to render it creation each time.)

Romans 8:20 refers back to the curse which God brought upon the creation as a consequence of the fall of humanity in the Garden of Eden (Genesis 3). But continuing with the personification of nature, Paul says it still has hope, the hope of full restoration at Christ's return. (Compare Acts 3:21: "Christ will restore everything.") It may be that only poets and artists can fully feel what Paul refers to here. The late Bishop Geo. R. Brunk (1871-1938), a sensitive theologian, spoke one time of "the ocean sobbing on the bosom of the shore." Paul is asserting that that sobbing will one glorious day cease! For the creation is destined in the matchless plan of redemption to be "liberated ... and brought into the glorious freedom of the children of God" (8:21). Note how different this is from the view of scientists that everything is running down: the suns of the universe are burning

out and the future is wholly bleak—it's only a question of time!
But Paul and the other apostles looked "forward to a new
heaven and a new earth" (2 Peter 3:13; Revelation 21:1). But that
glorious day has not yet come. The creation now is in distress; it
is "groaning" (8:22) like a woman in labor. Indeed, its several
parts *co-groan* (8:23)!

Christians Groan

For Paul Christians are in stage 1 of God's eternal salvation.
They now enjoy the full forgiveness of their sins; they are "born
again," having become partakers of the divine nature; they have
the righteousness of faith, perfect standing with God through
Christ; they are blessed with the "fruit of the Spirit"; God gives
them gifts of the Spirit according to the needs of the body of
Christ, the church; they bring their praises and their needs to a
prayer-hearing God; they have the assurance that God will both
begin in them, and continue until the end, granting to them
whatever strength and grace they may need to overcome the
world, the flesh, and the devil; they have the comfort and
strength which come from membership in the family of faith,
people with whom they can share as they both give and receive
counsel and affirmation; they meet together with those who are
Christ's to eat of the loaf and to drink from the fruit of the vine
in memory of the broken body and shed blood of their crucified
and resurrected redeemer; and they face the future with uplifted
face as they look for the day when their Lord will come for them.
Paul in this passage calls these rich spiritual blessings the "firstfruits of the Spirit" (8:23). Stages 2 and 3 of our salvation are still
future.

Christians enter stage 2 at the death of the body of humiliation, our lowly bodies; this is when we "depart [to] . . . be with
Christ, which is better by far" (Philippians 1:23) than remaining
in this life. And then fullness of salvation (stage 3) comes on "the
day of redemption" (Ephesians 4:30), that is the redemption of
our bodies (Romans 8:23). We now dwell in bodies which are
prone to weakness, illness, and doomed to die—unless we live

until the return of our Lord. Bishop George R. Brunk (1871-1938) estimated that he was ill about a thousand days in his busy life. John Calvin (1509-1563) suffered a multitude of ailments. A. B. Simpson (1844-1919), who had had twenty years of poor health and then was divinely healed so that he enjoyed a great thirty-five-year ministry, in the end had to endure a long and agonizing period of illness before he was released from this "lowly body." (He wrote some seventy books, including two on the Holy Spirit, as well as some beautiful hymns and poems, and founded the Christian and Missionary Alliance Church.)

But stage 3 of our glorious salvation in Christ will certainly be ours when our Lord returns for his own in all his glory, accompanied by myriads of angels; then the dead in Christ will be raised in redeemed bodies, fashioned like his body of glory, and we who are still alive at his coming will be changed in a moment, in the twinkling of an eye. Then we will have no further trouble with unredeemed bodies, but will enjoy the fullness of the blessings of the atonement of our Savior. And we will reign with him forever and ever. No wonder Paul calls our present blessings merely "the firstfruits of the Spirit"; he even admits that in this present situation we still groan (8:23); we join the unrestored creation as it groans! Bishop S. F. Coffman (1872-1954) once remarked with radiant face that there is "as much groaning in Romans 8 as in Romans 7." And think of the groaning in 2 Corinthians 5, along with our longing!

It is this hope of full deliverance from the present mortal body (8:23), and from all that is perishable and beset with weakness, which fills believers with holy joy. Christians hope and long for that which is not yet realized. We are saved now, but we live in the hope of the fullness of redemption, the reception of our glorified body. That hope is not yet realized. But it will be. For he will change this lowly body and make it conform to his own when he comes again for us. Thus Paul admits that we "groan inwardly" as we wait for our resurrection bodies, and he declares that we "wait eagerly" (8:23). After elaborating on this desire, he also remarks that "we wait for it patiently" (8:25).

The Spirit Groans

The creation groans, we Christians groan. Now Paul states
that in our bodily weakness we do not even know how to pray.
(We may have cancer, hardening of the arteries, or heart trouble.)
But the Holy Spirit, filled with love for us poor believers, comes
to our aid with petitions too deep for words. So he "intercedes
for us with groans that words cannot express" (8:26). What a
tremendous boost this awareness should give our weary spirits!
The Spirit is literally groaning for those of us who are still in
these lowly bodies, in bodies not yet glorified—but they surely
will be glorified when our Lord comes again. How comforting it
is to know that God, "who searches our hearts, knows the mind
of the Spirit" (8:27). He knows the meaning of these groans. God
knows what it is that we really need and for which the Spirit
groans. Indeed, it is God himself who wishes to bless us as we
have need. And "the Spirit intercedes for the saints in accordance
with God's will" (8:27). This is the ground of the assurance we
have that God is able to keep every believer unto a happy end in
Christ. Perseverance is just as much an act of God as is salvation
initially. It is God who moves us to repent. It is God who moves
us to the surrender of faith. It is God who gives to us overcoming
grace for each trial and testing. And it is God who will bring us
safely through all our tribulations. Praise his holy name!

God's Chain of Salvation

There are five great links in God's glorious chain of salvation: (1) Foreknowledge: we are "chosen according to the
foreknowledge of God the Father" (1 Peter 1:2); (2) Predestina-
tion: "he predestinated us to be adopted as his sons through
Jesus" (Ephesians 1:5); (3) Calling: our God has "called [us] . . .
out of darkness into his wonderful light" (1 Peter 2:9); (4) Justification: being declared righteous "through faith, we have peace
with God through our Lord Jesus Christ" (Romans 5:1). Those
are the four links which are already realized in the experience of
those who are Christians. But Paul moves on, for in God's sight
it takes all five links to form the golden chain of salvation. (5)

Glorification: this is stage 3 of divine salvation, when we are in heaven with God, glorified in the same way as our ascended and enthroned Lord Jesus (John 12:16)! This link is not yet realized, but in Paul's overview it is certain: link 1 leads directly to link 2, and so on to 5. Someone has called this the most daring step of faith in the New Testament!

Does this chain of salvation imply any sort of arbitrary election to faith? No, it doesn't. What it does say is that God knew his believing ones from all eternity; such believers are called the elect. This is the language of trust and praise. The invitation is still true: Whoever wills to come may do so! Perhaps three crisp statements will help us lay hold of the truth: Christ's atonement on Golgotha was adequate for all, it is offered to all, and it is intended for all. "Elect" often seems to mean that we are *precious* to God (L. Verduin).

God's Gracious Providence

We can best understand Romans 8:28 by examining what follows. There are two different readings here. The late manuscripts read: "All things work together for good to those who love God ... " (Compare the KJV). (This reading is supported by such manuscripts as Sinaiticus, C, D, and G.) The other reading, adopted by the NIV, reads: "And we know that in all things God works for the good of those who love him. . . . " (This reading is supported by the Chester Beatty Manuscript of about AD 200, by Vaticanus (B), and by various other authorities. Both Vaticanus and Sinaiticus were made in the fourth century, likely about AD 340, and where they differ, Vaticanus is perhaps slightly preferable.) This is not one of the easier questions to be settled by textual criticism, but I am inclined to keep God as the one who causes all things to work together for our good.

This verse does not teach fatalism. It does not say, "Whatever happens has been decreed by God; so do as you please, it is all bound to come out as God has planned it!" Rather, it is saying that what takes place is used by God for his eternal plan. To use one rare word we could say, It is used in God's "salvific" intention! God's concern is to see people become saved. He can use many things to bring them to repentance and life eternal. In no sense does Romans 8:28 relieve people of responsibility for their health and welfare—including their eternal welfare. Rather, it assures us of how eager God is to see us become his sons and daughters. We humans must assume total responsibility for what we do rather than live carelessly while appealing to Romans 8:28!

Our Security in Christ

If God is for us, who can be against us? (8:31). What does human opposition or even demonic hostility amount to if God is there "in our behalf" (this is the force of the Greek)? How do we know that God is there for us? The yardstick of God's love is Golgotha. He *did not spare his own Son* (8:32); he did not rescue Jesus who in human weakness cried to God to take the awful cup of suffering away from him, if possible. Rather, God allowed the Romans to crucify his son in behalf of us all. The Lord laid on him the iniquity of us all (Isaiah 53:6). And since he has given us a divine sin-bearer, "how will he not also . . . graciously give us all things?" (8:32). If God allowed his Son to die in our stead, will he withhold any trivial gift that we may need? If we ask in line with his holy will (1 John 5:14) he delights in showering his gifts upon us! Paul is stressing our spiritual security, for God is active in keeping us for eternal glory.

We turn from God as lavish giver to God as the one who pronounces us righteous against all the accusations of conscience, of Satan, and even of divine Law. *Who will bring any charge against those whom God has chosen?* (8:33). It is none other than the Almighty who pronounces us righteous! And who is able to pronounce condemnation? God has entrusted this task of judgment to only one man, Christ Jesus; he "has given proof of this to all men by raising him from the dead" (Acts 17:31). Our Lord is surely far from pronouncing condemnation on us. Rather he is "interceding for us" at the right hand of God (8:34).

Our future judgment is in the hands of him who is our Intercessor!

Neither seven nor seventeen dreaded items are able to separate us from Christ: Paul ticks off seven things which we humans fear: trouble, hardship, persecution, famine, nakedness, danger, and the sword (8:35). One has to wonder if he saved the one he most dreaded for last. Less than a decade later he was beheaded! He then thought of Psalm 44:22: "For your sake we face death all day long; we are considered as sheep to be slaughtered." Paul knew that just as Christ took up his cross, each true follower of Christ (in English, each true disciple) must likewise take up his cross, the individual cost of being a disciple (Luke 9:23). Hans Denk, a pitiably broken Anabaptist witness, said before his untimely death in 1527: "No one can truly know Christ except he follow him in life."

There was a secret source of sustenance and strength which Paul could not overlook: "we are more than conquerors through him who loved us" (8:37). Divine love encompasses, soothes, and sustains those who are facing death for Christ's sake. A missionary who faced death at the hands of a well-managed rabble in a foreign country, told me later that he never experienced Christ so closely as when he was put on public trial for his Lord.

But Paul has ten more dreadful things to mention: death, life, angels, demons, the present, the future, powers, height, depth, and anything else in all creation—none of them "will be able to separate us from the love of God that is in Christ Jesus our Lord" (8:39). Now that is real security!

Avoiding Misunderstandings

In dealing with a topic as serious as the eternal salvation of human beings, it is most important to avoid misunderstandings. There are voices in Christendom which cry: "Once a son, always a son!" "Once saved, always saved!" "We teach eternal security!" Are these sentiments biblical?

As far as God and his salvation are concerned, they are true. But it is also necessary to teach the duties which God has ordained for his children and the means by which he keeps his weak sons and daughters secure in faith. The Bible has many promises relating to the ability and intention of God to keep us in his family. There is no question about that. But it is also true that if we neglect prayer, Christian fellowship with God's saints, meditation on the Word of God, Christian stewardship, and witnessing, we may become so lukewarm, even cold, spiritually that we return to living according to the flesh. And if that happens, God's Word reminds us forcibly: we will die! (Romans 8:13). The worst example of an apostate is Judas, a man who was capable of becoming a mighty apostle in the primitive church, and yet who for a handfull of silver turned his teacher over to the Jewish authorities for ultimate crucifixion, and himself wound up a suicide. The New Testament mentions two other disciples by name who "shipwrecked their faith" (1 Timothy 1:19).

In other words, our security lies in faithfulness to the one who loved us and gave himself for us. It is a security in Christ, not in carelessness and sin. John 10 indicates that the Good Shepherd is able to keep his "sheep" who follow him. It is his will to keep us, but we have to follow! The Bible abounds in warnings like Hebrews 2:1: "We must pay more careful attention, therefore, to what we have heard, so that we do not drift away."

A number of years ago the outstanding Catholic radio minister, Msgr. Fulton J. Sheen, (1895-1979) told his radio audience that the church has many prelates (high-ranking clergymen) who in themselves were capable of becoming criminals. Then he went on to say that our prisons contain many criminals who in God were capable of becoming prelates in the church! The responsibility we bear for our eternal welfare is awesome. At the same time, eternal salvation is wholly of God and his grace. What a paradox!

Salvation Not by Assurance

Our security is in Christ and does not depend on our awareness of sonship or sense of Christian assurance—what the Germans call *Heilsgewissheit* (certainty of salvation). The faithful disciple, walking in love and holiness but lacking a robust sense of being in Christ, is a thousand times more certain of heaven than the loquacious showman who shouts about his salvation and his spiritual gifts, but who is notably lacking in personal integrity and down-to-earth spiritual brokenness and faithfulness. This can be illustrated by an Old Testament story: On the night of the exodus from Egypt, God had promised immunity from the death angel to every family who slew a lamb and sprinkled its blood on the doorposts and lintels of its house. All who were under the blood would be secure. It is entirely likely that the Israelites differed in the degree of peace and joy they felt that night. Possibly some families anxiously huddled together as the hour of the death angel's coming drew near. Perhaps others were singing "Glory, Glory, Hallelujah," knowing that they were safe. But all who were under the blood were, as a matter of fact, secure. Just so now: Everyone who turns from sin, makes the surrender of faith, and walks humbly with God, is secure. The degree of assurance felt by believers is bound to vary from one to another, but the reality of salvation is not dependent on one's feelings.

8

God and Israel

(Romans 9—11)

The Problem

Paul had been a Christian for well over twenty years when he wrote this epistle. But he had a problem. The question which haunted him unceasingly was the way the Jews in large numbers were turning down the Messiah (Christ in Greek), Jesus of Nazareth. These Jews were Paul's brethren and sisters, his kinfolk according to the flesh. Thinking about their unbelief caused Paul "great sorrow and unceasing anguish in [his] . . . heart" (9:2). So great was his love for his fellow-Jews that he could have wished himself to be "cut off from Christ for the sake of [his] . . . brothers" (9:3). The Jews had so many advantages spiritually: Paul mentions seven of them in 9:4-5: they had been adopted *as sons:* they had also received *divine glory, the covenants* (with Abraham, Isaac, Jacob, and, finally, with Moses), *the Law, the temple worship, and the promises,* particularly the messianic ones. Finally, from *them is traced the human ancestry of Christ:* (see Matthew 1); God gave Israel, as he had often promised, the Messiah (Hebrew) or Christ (Greek for the anointed one). Since Paul held firmly to the sovereignty of God over history, so the painful question for him was: How could a righteous God cast off his chosen people? This question takes up chapters 9, 10, and

11 of Romans. As an apostle filled with the Spirit of God, he is divinely led to four solutions: 1. God is sovereign; do not talk back to him. 2. God did not reject Israel; it was Israel who rejected God's plan of salvation. 3. Israel is not totally rejected; there is still a believing remnant. 4. Vast numbers of Israelites will yet turn to the Messiah!

Christ Both Man and God

Before we look at these four foundational principles, it is necessary to say a word about our Lord. In Romans 9:5 Paul looks at Christ both as human and divine and as *God.* Humanly, as to his family line ("flesh" in Greek), Christ's ancestry can be traced back to Abraham, Isaac, and Jacob (see Matthew 1:2). Christians believe in the incarnation (in German the *Menschwerdung* becoming human). That is, the eternal Son of God, in the greatest miracle of all history, literally was born of the Virgin Mary; grew up as a child and became a man; taught us the way of faith, love, and holiness, of justice and mercy; and finally died in our stead thus reconciling humanity to God (Romans 5:11; 2 Corinthians 5:18) and defeating Satan (Hebrews 2:14, 15). But Paul cannot stop with the humanity of our Lord. Because he is constrained to glory also in his deity, he adds that "Christ, who is God over all, forever [be] praised." Not all modern translations agree that the word "God" in 9:5 refers to Christ. However, Sanday and Headlam comment that "an immense preponderance of the Christian writers of the first eight centuries refer the word [God] to Christ," such as Irenaeus, Tertullian, Hippolytus, Cyprian, Athanasius, Gregory of Nyssa, Chrysostom, and Jerome. Sanday and Headlam add: "Moreover there is no evidence that this conclusion was arrived at on dogmatic grounds." Meyer adds such names as Augustine, Luther, Erasmus, and Calvin to those who support the interpretation given in the NIV. Many modern commentaries, however, see the phrase as a doxology to the Father, the one who sent the Messiah into the world. This also agrees with general apostolic usage. One of the most careful discussions of this verse is by Frederic Louis Godet (1812-1900),

the Swiss Evangelical Churchman. He sees this latter interpretation as switching from the Son to the Father as intolerably ab-
rupt. It "goes in the teeth of the feeling which has inspired the
whole passage thus far." The fact that Paul speaks of the human
ancestry of the Christ and then turns to the other predicate of our
Lord, his Deity, seems to call for the classic interpretation of the
Fathers, the Reformers, and some modern scholars. As to his
human nature, Christ was born a Jew; as to his divine nature, he
is God over all. Johann Peter Lange (1802-1884), after discussing
the sentence at length, concludes: "The strongest reasons are still
in favor of the old [interpretation], transmitted to us by the early
writers. . . . The passage is therefore a doxology to the divinity of
Christ."

We turn now to Paul's first foundational truth.

1. God Is Sovereign (Romans 9)

Paul reminds us first of all that "It is not as though God's
word had failed" (9:6). God never promised that every last Israelite would be a believer. Being a descendant of Abraham does
not make everyone an Israelite. Abraham had two sons, Ishmael
and Isaac: and God chose Isaac to be the father of the chosen
people. Isaac in turn had two sons, Jacob and Esau; and God in
his sovereignty chose the family of Jacob as his own. It is not
sheer biological sonship which counts before God; it is being
"the children of the promise" (9:8). The child born to Sarah
(Isaac) was the son of the divine promise (9:7-9).

Paul then considers the next generation, the sons born to
Isaac and Rebecca. Even before the sons were born, God chose
between the twins; in his sovereignty he designated Jacob as the
son of promise. Some expositors have too quickly, even carelessly, taken this passage to mean: "Jacob have I predestined to
eternal life, and Esau have I allowed to go to perdition." Bishop
Anders Nygren of Lund in Sweden insists that we look more
carefully both at this text and the Old Testament narrative to
which Paul appeals. (See his *Romarbrevet,* 1944, and the English
translation of 1949, by the Muhlenberg Press, *Commentary on*

Romans.) The passage in question reads, "The older will serve the younger." Just as it is written: "Jacob I loved, but Esau I hated" (9:12-13). Let us look carefully at this language.

In order to penetrate to the true meaning of these words, these facts must be considered: First, it is a Hebrew idiom to use *hated* to mean "to give second place to." Compare the words of our Lord on hating earthly relatives in order to give first place to Christ (Luke 14:26). Second, a careful reading of Genesis 25 indicates that it is nations (Edom versus Israel) which is the real point of the contrast. Third, the passage has to do with relative significance in history, not with destiny in eternity. God would use Israel, not Edom, to give the Scriptures and the Messiah to humanity. Four, it would be utterly inappropriate to charge God with unrighteousness (9:14)!

Paul also points out that God's sovereignty does not apply only to his choice of the patriarchs, but also to the ability of God to use wicked old Pharaoh for his glory—although Pharaoh did not know that he was advancing God's gracious intention for Israel. The *hardening* (9:17-18) of Pharaoh by God was judicial in character: First, Pharaoh hardened his own heart (Exodus 8:15, 8:32; 9:12; 10:20). Furthermore, what sinful human being would be so arrogant as to set up a standard of righteousness by which to measure the God of mercy and grace? (9:20). God is the great potter, and we are but the clay in his hands (9:21). The entire body of believers, both Jewish and Gentile, have been recipients of the infinite love and mercy of God (9:23, 24). Further, Paul cannot allow an opportunity to pass to show from Scripture to his radically proud fellow-Jews the full right of the Gentiles to be members of the Messiah's church! Therefore, he quotes from Hosea 2:23; 1:10; Isaiah 10:22, 23; 1:9; 8:14; and 28:16, patiently proving that God planned all along for the Gentiles to be in the church, while only a remnant of Israel will be saved (Romans 9:25-29). The amazing fact is that although the Gentiles did not initially *pursue righteousness* (the Greek verb means to pursue with a passion; in some cases it means to persecute), many now have the *righteousness* which comes by *faith* (9:30). On the other

hand, Israel did pursue *righteousness* with great earnestness, only
to miss it entirely, for they sought righteousness by *works,* that is,
by merit (9:31-32). In the last quotation (9:33) Paul follows the
Septuagint (the Greek version of the Hebrew Scriptures made
about 285-135 BC), even though it deviates a bit from the Hebrew of Isaiah 8:14 and 28:16. (Paul takes up Israel's fatal mis-
take in Romans 10.)

2. God Did Not Reject Israel (Romans 10)

Our Lord and his apostles had to labor hard to try to eradi-
cate from the Jewish mind the idea of works of merit. Here again
Paul stresses that "Christ is the end [fulfillment] of the law": that
is, no one becomes righteous before God by achievement (10:4).
Rather, God asks for the submission of faith. Thus, the failure of
so many of the Jews was that they paid no attention to the terms
of the good news, for God asks for repentance and the surrender
of faith. The Greek verb which Paul used (10:3) really means "to
be ignorant of" or "not to know"; but practically it could mean
"not to recognize" or "to disregard" (Arndt-Gingrich, 11). The
Jews attempted the route of self-effort and failed to attain God's
salvation. There is only one route which can carry one to the
total well-being called "salvation" in the New Testament. The
way to salvation is the way of faith: righteousness by faith as set
forth in Romans 1:17 and 3:21-31. It appears that this truth is
harder for "religious" people to grasp than for the irreligious!

If salvation were a matter of merit, of conforming to law,
then the way would be clear: "the man who does these things
[commands] will live by them" (10:5). But the way of the good
news is altogether different; Paul calls it the "Word of faith"
(10:8). "That if you confess with your mouth, 'Jesus is Lord,' and
believe in your heart that God raised him from the dead, you will
be saved" (10:9). How simple and clear! And yet how difficult for
proud human nature which wants to achieve! Paul says once
more that as a result of believing, one is declared righteous (justified), and the act of confession ("My faith is in Jesus") brings
salvation (10:10). God hears Jews and Gentiles alike (10:12). In

his usual manner Paul quotes the Old Testament in support of his doctrine and ethic (10:13), in this case Joel 2:32, also using the Septuagint. In the Septuagint Kyrios without the article is used to translate the Hebrew name of Israel's covenant Lord, possibly Jahweh in form. (No vowels were written in Hebrew.) Thus Paul sees Jesus as the full revelation of Jahweh and quotes a Jahweh passage to justify looking to Jesus for salvation. This is standard New Testament practice. Whenever the Lord is referred to in the Old Testament, it meant Jahweh; but when the New Testament refers to the present Lord, the reference is to the Lord Jesus Christ. This is really not a total surprise, since it is a well-known fact that the apostolic church held to the full deity (as well as the full humanity) of the incarnate Son of God.

Romans 9:14-15 points out how important it is for the church to commission witnesses to the good news so that people may learn how to call on the name of the Lord and put their faith in the Lord Jesus, our Savior and redeemer. "How beautiful are the feet of those who bring good news!" In this case the good news was the gospel of Christ.

Paul closes this part of the discourse by quoting several Scriptures on how stubbornly Israel resisted the gospel, as had been prophesied, but how the Gentiles would openly respond to the good news of Christ!

3. Israel Is Not Totally Rejected (Romans 11:1-10)

Paul has several key concepts which he delights in repeating. One of them is the joyful response to the good news of salvation in Christ by the surrender of faith, a message of free grace which the merit-minded Jews found hard to accept but strangely enough which the Gentiles seemed to welcome. Another is the constant reminder that God has always had a believing remnant. The situation was no different when Paul wrote to the Romans. In fact, he himself was a sample of the believing remnant in Israel. God had never rejected his covenant people, even though many of them had rejected the gospel of Christ! Paul points out that he himself was an Israelite, descended from Abraham, the

father of the faithful, and a member of the tribe of Benjamin
(11:1). Paul reminds his readers how tragic the situation appeared to Elijah, the prophet of old who actually thought that he
was the only man of true faith left! But what was the answer of
the all-knowing God of the covenant? God told Elijah that he
still had 7,000 true believers left in Israel in Elijah's day (11:2-4).
Who would have thought that in the dark era of Ahab and Jez-
ebel God would still have had a faithful remnant of 7,000 believers?

And so it was even in Paul's day. God still had his chosen
remnant; although Paul did not know their number, he knew
that there were Jewish believers. And each one of the remnant
was a believer by the grace of God. All believers are! And those
who refuse the grace of God, offered them in the gospel, are
spiritually hardened (11:7); they find the voice of the Spirit, who
seeks to nudge them toward conversion, growing more and more
dim. This is the law of sowing and reaping at work. And it is
God's law. God has made it clear in his Word: he does not want
anyone to perish spiritually. He wishes all to be saved. As people
obey the nudgings of the Spirit, they hear him with ever sharper
hearing. But if they disobey they become more and more subject
to a "spirit of stupor." They no longer care about their spiritual
state. They have brought this condition on themselves, yet it is
also God's punishment for their rejection of the light. Judas is an
example. There was a time when he showed bright promise of
spiritual victory, but he allowed the love of money to kill all his
capacities for growth. And finally, he left for the fateful field with
a coil of rope.

4. Vast Numbers of Israelites Will Yet Turn to the Messiah
(Romans 11:11-32).

Paul began this section (9—11) of his letter with a woeful
cry of heart anguish. If only something could be done for his
beloved Jewish brethren who refuse to bow their hearts to the
blessed Lord Jesus! Now comes the full revelation of what the
Spirit of God led him to as he wrestled with the problem.

First of all, one of the good outcomes of this Jewish rejection is the way the gospel then came to be offered to the Gentiles in one city after another across the Roman Empire (11:11). This observation by Paul should not be elevated to a point of theology: Paul is not saying that had large numbers of Jews accepted Jesus as the Messiah, the gospel invitation would never have been extended to the Gentiles. Rather, Paul looks back over the way the gospel had begun to spread across the Roman Empire, and he recalls one city after another where Jewish opposition compelled the missioners to "turn to the Gentiles."

Second, Paul expressed the hope that the entrance of many Gentiles into the Messiah's kingdom might stir in Israel a spirit of jealousy or envy (11:11). (The verb used here means to provoke to jealousy, or to make jealous. It can even mean to make angry; see Arndt-Gingrich, 621). It is a human characteristic that when we see people laying hold of a precious offer, we too want to "get in on the act." Paul hoped that when the Jews saw Gentiles streaming into the divine kingdom, they too might be stirred into action and thus come to Jesus for salvation. This miracle would magnify the riches of divine grace, if the Jews would turn to God through Christ in fullness (which likely means, "in substantial numbers" 11:12).

Third, God had to reject so many Jews because they refused submission to his Son, thereby promoting the salvation of large numbers of Gentiles. Thus the acceptance of the Jews when they do turn to Christ will be as great a miracle as a resurrection from the dead (11:15). And God yearns for precisely this spiritual turning of Abraham's seed to Christ in penitence and faith. The Jews have every right to come to Jesus, for they have as their "root" such great patriarchs of faith as Abraham, Isaac, and Jacob. They are therefore already "holy" in the sense of belonging to a people whom God chose in Abraham to be his special treasure. To make this come alive, Paul uses two simple illustrations: how yeast works through an entire batch of dough, and how a tree sends sap from its roots to its branches. Both as part of God's dough and as branches of God's tree, Israel's spiritual sustenance has not been taken from them by God. In God's intention, Israel still rightfully belongs to her holy God (11:16).

Fourth, Paul elaborates on his tree illustration. God has a holy olive tree, says Paul. The entire tree was originally Jewish in character, but because so many Israelites turned from God in unbelief and disobedience, God had to break off those disobedient branches. In their place (Gentiles, please note!) God grafted in wild olive branches, the Gentiles, so that the tree of faith might be filled out (11:17). But Gentiles must always remember that it was they who were grafted into the tree; believing Jews were not grafted into a Gentile tree! It is the Jewish roots and tree which support the believing Gentiles (11:18). And there is no place for Gentile arrogance or pride, for if God could remove the disobedient Jewish branches from the holy olive tree, he could also remove unworthy Gentile branches which were not there in the first place! "Do not be arrogant, but be afraid. For if God did not spare the natural branches, he will not spare you either" (11:20, 21).

Fifth. "Consider therefore the kindness and sternness of God: sternness to those who fell," to the Jews who refused the surrender of faith. (The Arndt-Gingrich Greek *Lexicon* gives "severity" as the best rendering of the Greek word translated as "sternness" in the NIV; it is used only here in all the New Testament.) But kindness (or goodness, generosity according to Arndt-Gingrich) is granted to you who believe—followed by the conditional if—if "you continue in [God's] . . . kindness" (or goodness). "Otherwise, you also will be cut off," Gentiles! (11:22). And the Jews also—now another conditional if—"if they do not persist in unbelief, they will be grafted in, for God is able to graft them in again (11:23). And what would be more natural than for God to graft the cultivated olive branches back into their place, the place which had been occupied by the grafted-in wild olive branches? (11:24).

Sixth, Paul now let's us in on a divine secret, what is called a "mystery" in the New Testament. God will yet save vast numbers of Jews. "Israel has experienced a hardening in part until the full number of the Gentiles has come in," that is, into the body of Christ, the church (11:25). In the economy of God, he first used the Jews to give a witness to the unity and oneness of the Godhead, what theologians call "monotheism." Also, the Jews were supposed to give a witness, not only against polytheism, but also against the giving of veneration to visible representations of various deities, as well as representations of the one true God: that is, against all idolatry. The first of the Ten Commandments calls upon Israel to worship the one true God alone. The second forbids making any sort of idol. God also gave the Scriptures (what we now call the Old Testament) through Israel's prophets and poets. And finally, the Messiah came into the world through a Jewish maiden named Mary.

Now, says Paul, it is evident that the church of this day is largely Gentile in character—the pendulum of God's effectual call has swung to the Gentiles. However, in due time the pendulum of God's great clock of grace will again swing back to the literal descendants of Abraham, the Jews. But first the fullness of the Gentiles must come into the body of Christ by repentance and faith, by claiming the salvation offered in the good news. "And so all Israel will be saved" (11:26). The *so* is an adverb of manner; it could be rendered, "thus." And thus by believing on the Messiah, first the "fullness" or "full number of the Gentiles" will come into Christ's fold, and then the fullness (11:12) of the Jews will follow: "and so all Israel" both the cultivated and the wild olive branches, "will be saved" (11:26). The "Israel of God" is made up of believing Jews and believing Gentiles (Galatians 6:16). The two groups have already been merged into one body (Ephesians 2:14). But the Christian church should work and pray for the day when vast numbers of Jews are also gathered into the church of the Lord.

At this point Paul breaks into poetry, quoting from Isaiah the prophet. "The deliverer will come from Zion"; that is, he will be Jewish by race. *He will* "turn godlessness away from Jacob"; that is, Christ will bring penitence and trust and true piety to Israel. And God will effect his "covenant with them when [he takes] . . . away their sins" (11:26, 27).

At the present time, says Paul, the Jews are still largely hostile to their Messiah, for the pendulum of grace is at the moment over the Gentiles. "But as far as election is concerned", God, who loves with an eternal love, still has his plan to make the pendulum swing back over the family of Abraham, Isaac, and Jacob, for the Jews "are loved on account of the patriarchs" (11:28). At this point Paul falls back on his doctrine of an almighty God: "for God's gifts [the word might be translated grace-gifts or free gifts] and his call [or calling to become his child through Christ] are irrevocable" (11:29). God's grace was evident in his calling of many Gentiles; and God's grace will also be evident as he calls many Jews! (11:31, 32).

Paul's struggle of faith is over. He now sees what he may never have seen so clearly before. He now realizes afresh how great the redeeming love and mercy of God are. Thus what began as a groan, as pain in the heart, ends with a glorious song of praise, praise to God as the author of the marvelous plan of salvation (11:33-36):

> Oh, the depth of the riches of the wisdom
>   and knowledge of God!
>   How unsearchable his judgments,
>   and his paths beyond tracing out!
> "Who has known the mind of the Lord?
>   Or who has been his counselor?"
> "Who has ever given to God,
>   that God should repay him?"
> For from him and through him and to him are all things.
>   To him be the glory forever! Amen.

9

The Transformed Disciple

(Romans 12—13)

Heart Holiness: 12:1, 2

After Paul's moving doxology at the end of Romans 11, he looks back over God's total work for us: providing a Savior and Mediator, by his Spirit moving us to turn from sin and to make the surrender of faith, forgiving us all our sins, granting to us by his grace full acceptance and declaring us to be righteous, and assuring us that he will keep us to a happy end in Christ. And now, declares the Apostle, it is only right that Christians should respond to the compassion or mercy of God. And how shall we respond? The appropriate response, says Paul, is to come before God with a gift-sacrifice. In the old covenant, this sacrifice was an animal which was slain. But now in the new covenant, says Paul, we are not to offer to our holy God a dead animal. Rather, we are to bring to him a living sacrifice—ourselves! Our sacrifice is to be holy (set apart to belong to God), and we are assured that it is indeed pleasing to our God. This bringing of ourselves to God, in contrast with the material form of worship (animal sacrifices) of the old covenant, is a spiritual form of worship. That which is offered to God is the joyful putting of ourselves at his disposal. "Lord, what would you wish me to do?" (The Greek word rendered "reasonable" in the KJV is better rendered "spiritual".) The first step in our response to all that our holy God has done for us in his "incredible" love, as one writer calls it, is to make a total surrender to him.

The second step is to stop patterning ourselves (we are not to co-pattern ourselves) according to this world (12:2). (Some people insist on using the word "age" rather than "world." But in the English idiom, in a context like Romans 12, the best English equivalent is world.) One of the happiest phrases at this point is by the translator, Dr. J. B. Phillips, who urges the readers not to allow the world around them to squeeze them into its own mold! The world puts a high premium on physical pleasure, wealth, creature comforts, the gratifying of the desires of the natural man (he who is not born again), recognition or praise for achievements, and so on. The worldly man wants his own way. But the child of God is concerned to know and to do the will of God. He is not a martyr by desire, nor an ascetic, but he does look upon all earthly pleasures as being secondary. He does not live for thrills; he lives rather for the glory of God.

The spiritual Christian may farm, or work with his hands as a carpenter (Jesus did), or in a profession (Zenas was a lawyer); he may get married and have childen; he may own property. And yet he exercises a certain restraint about all these things; he does not allow either family or occupational concerns to have top priority in his life. This is surely what Paul meant when he told the Corinthians (1 Corinthians 7:29-31) to live in relative detachment from this world with its business and pleasures.

The third helpful instruction is that believers are to be "transformed (metamorphosed) by the renewing of [the] . . . mind" (12:2). That is, they are to surrender to God so fully that by his Spirit he will be able to mold them into the mind of the Spirit, that is, the mind of Christ. His goals are their goals, his disappointments are theirs, his joys are theirs; what he loves they love, what is offensive to him displeases them. As he is minded, so are they—as they daily and hourly give themselves to him and open themselves to his leading.

The gross sins of the flesh are ruled out for the child of God;

injustice, adultery, immorality in any form, carnality, hatred, vengeance, toying with the occult, profanity. The great spiritual leaders from Cyprian (martyred 260) through Francis of Assisi (died 1226), Menno (died 1561), John Woolman (died 1772), and John Wesley (died 1791) were concerned about the poor of this world and the sinful manner in which the powerless of society were exploited by the rich. They were concerned for justice in society. The very worst, the system of this world which most degraded human beings created in the image of God, was human slavery, and the evils it brought with it. John Woolman refused to wear dyed cloth, for the dye depended on slave labor. In general we may note that minorities are often exploited by the dominant group in any society. Majorities do not hesitate to use force to keep minorities "in their place."

When a strong minority sees the evil which society is nurturing, it is tempted to resort to force in the name of justice. But one evil is not conquered by another evil. Christians need to recall the apostle Paul's reminder to the Corinthians that "though we live in the world, we do not wage war as the world does. The weapons we fight with are not the weapons of the world. On the contrary, they have divine power to demolish strongholds" (2 Corinthians 10:3, 4). The world has not yet learned this; perhaps it never will. Governments can even kill people while trying to get them to treat other people with love! Christians have much more powerful "arms" or means: they bring about vast social changes by holy living, loving witnessing, and fervent praying. One of the more daring witnesses in our day has been Clarence Jordan (1912-1969) who established the Koinonia Farms of Americus, Georgia, in an effort to show that one can live in loving relations with blacks; one can work for justice without resorting to violence to try to suppress violence. If the Christian church should conclude that wholesale abortions are unvarnished sin, it would not be appropriate to bomb the hospitals which are guilty of committing such sin, but it would be very much in order to appeal quietly to the American conscience with fasting and prayer to cease and desist from the taking of human life in any form:

abortion, warfare, capital punishment, or euthanasia.

Further, Christians should not wait to give their witness until majority opinion happens to support their cause. God's real witnesses are like Athanasius (296-372) of Alexandria, Egypt. He was a lifelong witness to the deity of our Lord. Five times he was imperially banished; he spent a total of twenty of his forty-six years as a bishop in exile. One time he was told that the whole world was against him (which, as usual, in such remarks, was not altogether true). His reply was simply, "Then I am against the world!" His phrase, in Latin, *contra mundum,* became a well-known one down through church history. Philip Schaff, the Swiss American scholar, called Bishop Athanasius "one of the purest, most imposing, and venerable personages in the history of the church." Because he had opened himself up fully to witness faithfully for our Lord, Athanasius is honored by all Christ's true witnesses.

Unity in Diversity: 12:3-8

Before Paul discusses the variety of gifts in the church, he has a few introductory remarks to make. The first is, Look out for conceit! With his tender shepherd's heart, Paul does not rave and rant against conceit, how it ruins spiritual effectiveness. Rather, he suggests to each member of the church at Rome that it would be ill-advised to be carried away with self-conceit; it would be much better to be sober-minded! For just as God put the several members into the one human body, so also in his sovereignty he places numerous gifts in the church. He knows what he is doing, and he knows what is needed in the body, both in the human body and also in the body of Christ. God has given a "measure of faith" (12:3) to each member, and each member plays his unique role in the church. "Each member belongs to all the others" (12:5). Not exhaustively, but by way of illustration, Paul enumerates seven gifts of divine grace: (12:6-8) (1) Some Christians are gifted in the field of *prophesying:* speaking by the Spirit; those who prophesy strengthen, encourage, and comfort others. (2) Some are gifted in the area of *ministering:* like Jesus, they go about doing good. (3) Some are gifted in the area of *teaching:* they are able to make the truth plain, to make it "live." (4) Some are gifted in *encouraging* others: they know how to exhort others, how to get them into action. (5) Others are gifted in their ability to *contribute* to the needs of others, to share with them. (6) Some are gifted in the area of *leadership;* they preside well; this gift could refer to those who are overseers or deacons. Perhaps today we would say they are gfited in the area of administration. (7) Finally, Paul mentions the way some are gifted in *showing mercy:* they know how to live by love and to manifest a cheerful heart in doing so.

Paul is not saying that these several gifts of divine grace are special creations of the Spirit, nor is he saying that people were simply "made that way." Perhaps it is somewhat like different kinds of light fixtures, all of which need to be connected with the electrical source in order to shed their light. The members of the body of Christ need to be filled with the Spirit of God in order to be of maximum blessing to his Church. It is the Spirit who knows how to overcome the ugliness of raw human nature, and how to cause to spring to life those blessings which are sorely needed in the family of faith. But the greatest gift is still to be mentioned.

The Gift of Agapé Love: 12:9-16

It is no Spirit-gift to pretend to have caring love. "Love must be sincere" (12:9). God must pour his love into our hearts, so that we are genuinely concerned about the needs and the welfare of others. This Greek word for love is the highest type of unselfish affection, of genuine caring. It is not romantic love, but the caring of one whose heart God has touched and transformed. It has nothing to do with an effusive or gushing type of shallowness. It is a deep, unselfish, divine type of affection or caring.

We are to "hate (this word is used only here in the Greek New Testament) [or abhor] what is evil; to cling to what is good" (12:9). These are genuine opposites. And these attitudes are natural for the one who is filled with God's good Spirit.

"Be devoted to one another in brotherly love. Honor one

another above yourselves" (12:10). We are eager to do what we know will be helpful to the other members of Christ's body. We gladly give honor and recognition to them, giving them encouragement and affirmation. We are, if filled with the Spirit, generous in our words of appreciation. What a beautiful church life that makes possible!

"Never be lacking in zeal, but keep your spiritual fervor, serving the Lord" (12:11). ("Not slothful in business" is a poor rendering.) One of the worst ways to live the Christian life is to be halfhearted about it. But we know how the Lord hates lukewarmness: He has informed us that such people are most distasteful to him (Revelations 3:16).

"Be joyful in hope" (12:12). Christians may face the future with hope because God is in control. The next big event in the history of the world is the return of God's Son, Jesus Christ. This is the hope of the church, for it will mark the end of all trials, temptations, persecutions, and hardships of the people of God. And we know that God's grace is going to be more than adequate for any difficulties that may come in the meantime.

"Patient in affliction" (12:12). The word translated "patient" is that sturdy virtue which bears up through thick and thin; it is quiet endurance; it has staying power when the times are hard for Christian disciples. What if Paul or Silas had abandoned their missionary witness the moment they were beaten or stoned or imprisoned?

"Faithful in prayer" (12:12). Prayer is the God-given means of dealing with issues, and obtaining grace and strength for trials, of undergirding other disciples and ourselves for the battles of life. It is also a delightful and sanctifying communion with God through Jesus Christ, in the power of the Holy Spirit. It is however typically and tragically human that we sometimes imagine that we are too busy to pray. That is exactly when we ought to pray the more. And prayer is so much more than a "Give me" attitude. It is adoration, intercession, thanksgiving, supplication, and the bowing of the heart in fresh submission. We need it—crucially.

"Share with God's people who are in need" (12:13). Because love is the earmark of being a true child of God, love is ready to share, even to the point of personal suffering. Gifts of love to those in need are therefore normal in the Christian life. Such mutual support binds the members of the church together in love. It is the exact opposite of the selfish attitude which declares: "This money is mine; I made it, and no one has any right to it. Let such people earn like I do, and let them learn to manage." Such an attitude is harsh and betrays a cold heart. A Spirit-filled Christian simply cannot take such a heartless attitude.

"Practice hospitality" (12:13). The Greek word for "practice" is a strong one, and means to pursue with vigor; it can even mean "to persecute." We Westerners could learn much from the Near East. Historically, it was unthinkable to fail to take in the traveler and share with him your humble meal, even to give up your bed so that he might get a good rest! To a large extent this was also true of the rural background of many readers of this book. It was unthinkable to visit a congregation of "like faith" and not to receive several invitations to dinner. Though uninvited, people would drop in to eat with loved ones—for they knew how pleased the host and hostess would be. Many a time the family saw a Christian family coming in the lane after the table was already set; immediately, plans were changed and extra boards were put into the table. (How can we North American Christians regain lost ground? Are we ashamed to eat simply? Do we have to impress people with our ability to put on a sumptuous meal? Why not eat in the style of Doris Janzen Longacre's *More-with-Less Cookbook,* published by Herald Press?)

"Bless those who persecute you; bless and do not curse" (12:14). We should not think that the apostle is telling us to do what is exactly contrary to our nature, but it is a reminder that at all times the Christian needs to follow the impulses of the divine nature which the Holy Spirit has implanted in him. The Christian must also reckon as dead those impulses of human nature which run counter to those of the Spirit. Note how vividly this pair of impulses—of the flesh and of the Spirit—are contrasted in Galatians 5:16-25. It is when the Holy Spirit is continually given the right to be in control that the believer experiences liberation from law. He is then no longer under law ("I must not, dare not, do this or that"); he is above law ("I delight to do the will of God; it is a challenge to show love to those who seek to make me suffer, or even to die"). Only love can convert a hating persecutor into a loving and broken disciple of Jesus. Note the beautiful prayer of Christ's Spirit-filled martyr, Stephen (Acts 7:60), and the moving words of the Lord Jesus when he was being spiked to the cross (Luke 23:34).

"Rejoice with those who rejoice; mourn with those who mourn" (12:15). Paul is telling us to feel with people. The word sympathy comes from two Greek words, "to suffer" and "with," roughly to "co-suffer." Here Paul urges us both to *rejoice* with those who have been blessed and to *weep* with those suffering because of misfortune, pain, or the death of a loved one. We human beings are emotional creatures; nothing draws us to someone as much as knowing that he is right there with us, sharing our troubles or rejoicing at our good fortune. We do these things not because God has decreed that we shall, but because we do care; we rejoice because the good fortune of the one we love makes us happy, and the suffering of the one who is weeping touches our hearts.

The next Greek phrase is somewhat cryptic but can be rendered as, "Live in harmony with one another" (12:16). More literally it reads: "The same thing toward others being minded." Luther put it like this: *"Habt einerlei Sinn untereinander"* (Have one sort of mind among yourselves). The Froschauer Swiss Bible reads much the same : "Have one sort of disposition and mind among yourselves." (The Swiss here employed *hendiadys,* two words for a single complex idea.) Perhaps Paul is warning against such things as displaying wealth on one occasion, poverty on another; sophistication with one group of people, simple faith with others. What follows seems to support this interpretation. It might be rendered literally: do not set your mind on lofty or proud things, "but be willing to associate with people of low position." In other words, Be a consistently humble disciple of the lowly Nazarene. The last phrase in the paragraph might be paraphrased, "Don't seek to give the impression that you are sophisticated." The KJV has: "Be not wise in your own conceits." The NIV reads: "Don't be conceited." Luther is closer to the above paraphrase: "*Haltet euch nicht selbst für klug*" (Do not regard yourselves as clever). This brief admonition is a clear call to look out for conceit!

How to Deal with Unjust Suffering: 12:17-21

Someone has remarked somewhat bitterly that the history of theology is the account of how theologians have tried to escape from the Sermon on the Mount! I have a vivid memory of the day when a group of Mennonites and a group of NAE (National Association of Evangelicals) members spent a couple days searching the Word of God together and discussing the issues of peace and war for Christians. In response to a presentation calling for the Christian disciple to be a nonresistant sufferer rather than a killer for his country, the able spokesman for those who did not take the peace position made a most remarkable statement. As nearly as I can recall, he said something to this effect: "I grant that if one simply takes the New Testament teaching, it means adopting the nonresistant position." However, the same speaker went on to declare that the Old Testament saints went to war, and nonresistance is simply not practical! But that is precisely the question. Shall we adopt the position which seems to be necessary for self-defense, or shall we obey at any cost what Jesus Christ taught?

If we can trust the best research available—scholars such as Roland H. Bainton, Harold S. Bender, Cecil John Cadoux, William R. Durland, Melvin Gingerich, Adolf von Harnack, Guy F. Hershberger, John Horsch, Jean Michel Hornus, Culbert G. Rutenber, E. J. Swalm, John A. Toews, and John H. Yoder—the Christian writers, prior to Constantine the Great in the early fourth century, with one accord held to nonresistance. The most learned and ancient defense of peace and nonresistance was given by the mighty Origen (c.185-c.254).This was also the position of Waldo of South France (died c. 1217), of Peter Chelcicky of Bohemia (died c. 1457), of the Swiss Anabaptist such as Conrad Grebel (died 1526) and Michael Sattler (martyred 1527); of South German Anabaptists such as Pilgram Marpeck (died 1556), and of peaceful Frisian Anabaptists such as Jacob Van Campen (died 1535), Menno Simons (died 1561), and Dirk Phillips (died 1568). The Society of Friends (Quakers) held to the same position from their founding about 1647, as did the German Baptists (now Church of the Brethren) since 1708. What does the Word of God teach: the duty of self-defense, coupled with participation in the military? or the way of the cross, nonresistant suffering—the way of Jesus Christ and the New Testament?

"Do not repay anyone evil for evil. Be careful to do what is right in the eyes of everybody" (12:17). Paul is realistic; since he knew that not everyone can be won by love, that some people will remain hostile no matter how loving one is, he added: "If it is possible, so far as it depends on you, live at peace with everybody" (12:18). Following love did not spare most of the twelve disciples form martyrdom, not to mention Christ himself, nor Paul.

"Do not take revenge, my friends, but leave room for God's wrath, for it is written: 'It is mine to avenge; I will repay,' says the Lord. On the contrary: 'If your enemy is hungry, feed him; if he is thirsty, give him something to drink. In doing this, you will heap burning coals on his head.' Do not be overcome by evil, but overcome evil with good" (12:19-21).

As mentioned already, many individual Christians and Christian groups have taken literally, at face value, these verses from Romans 12. They have held that disciples of Christ should, like their Lord, be ready to pay any price in order to walk in this way of suffering love and nonresistance. It should also be noted that it is not a matter of ethical hairsplitting—"how far" to take these verses. Rather, if we take them at all, can we participate in modern warfare and killing? Beyond killing with the sword and with bullets, we now have such demonic ways of killing as nuclear warheads, blockbuster bombs, and incendiaries which kindle fierce fires that water cannot quench, as well as napalm weapons of destruction which burn people to a crisp. Agents of defoliation may do vast damage to the genetic pool that could last millenniums. Not to mention poison gas, germ warfare, nerve gas, and the like! And along with modern armies goes a scourge of drug abuse and veneral diseases. Again we say, the question is not how far to take Romans 12 and the Sermon on the Mount; it is rather, if we follow such portions of God's Word at all, can we participate in modern warfare?

How grateful nonresistant Christians are to such countries as England, Canada, France, West Germany, the United States, Mexico, Italy, the Netherlands, and various other lands which recognize that there are sincere people whose consciences, like that of Luther at the Diet of Worms in 1521, are captive to the Word of God. In the case of Luther, that meant holding to the gospel of grace through faith. In the case of Christian conscientious objectors, it means the unwillingness for conscience' sake to take human life in any way, shape, or form.

O Lord, give us the mind of Christ!

The Submissive Citizen: Romans 13:1-7

The NIV attempts to give the reader the same impression as the original readers got from the text. The Greek says, "Let every soul be in subjection to the high or superior authorities." The Arndt-Gingrich Greek Lexicon correctly explains that what the words really mean is, "those in authority." Also, since we do not today speak of people as "souls," the NIV reads: "Everyone must submit himself to the governing authorities" (13:1). Once again, Luther hits the nail on the head: *"Jedermann sei untertan der Obrigkeit"* (Let everyone be in subjection to the govenment). This subjection is not qualified by the character or the wisdom in governing of those in authority. For example, King Herod Agrippa II lived in incest with his sister Bernice—and considerable scandal built up around this relationship. But when the apostle Paul stood before him, Paul made no mention of the scandal. Paul addressed him with courtesy and respect—not because of his character, but simply because he was the king.

Likewise, when Paul wrote Romans, the emperor was none other than Nero, who was himself a hard man. He murdered his stepbrother Britannicus so that he might become the ruling Caesar. (The emperor Claudius had died of poison the fall of AD 54.) Nero is described as "a monster of lust and cruelty," and his wickedness was progressively revealed. He reigned only until 68 AD; then he, too, ended his life. (He tried to commit suicide but had to call on a supporter to complete his self-destruction.) There were a number of uncomplimentary things Paul could have written about Nero, but he was not writing on the virtues which ought to adorn an emperor; rather, he was discussing what sort of attitude Christians ought to take toward those in the government. That attitude can be expressed in one word: Submission! "For there is no authority except that which God has established" (13:1). It is not said here that God is pleased by a person getting to the throne by the murder of his rivals. It is not asserted that all a monarch may do is in itself pleasing to God. It is a bit like marriage, as the late Edward Yoder (1893-1945) helped us to see. God may not be pleased by the establishment of a given home; he certainly does not approve of the attitudes in some homes, nor of their way of life. But what God does approve is the institution of marriage.

The case of government is similar. God may be displeased by how the monarch got to the throne; and his way of governing may be cruel and despotic and therefore not according to the love and justice of God Almighty. But what is approved by God is the institution of government. Further, God's sovereignty must also be recognized: either God's directive will has been followed, or his permissive will has allowed a given ruler to ascend to the throne and to do this or that harsh thing.

Indeed, we can take one more step. The kind of ruler a given society of people puts on the throne can illustrate the law of sowing and reaping, for that is God's law. God can punish a people through his law of sowing and reaping by allowing them to establish an unjust ruler over them. Or God's law of sowing and reaping can bless a people by allowing them to put on the throne a person who works for civil justice and other good things.

"Consequently, he who rebels against the authority is rebelling against what God has instituted" (13:2). The Greek word for "rebel" means to oppose or to resist, and Paul remarks that those who resist will bring (human) judgment on themselves. However, Paul also indicates that to resist the authorities is after all to set oneself up against a divine institution. Having said that, he moves on to the terror that a rebel may experience, since rulers are aware of the resistance. The answer, Paul assures us, is to do that which is good; then we will have nothing to fear. On the contrary, the ruler will commend the good citizen. The ruler is, in fact, God's minister or servant (the word is used a few times of a "deacon") to you for good, or as the NIV renders it, "he is God's servant to do you good (13:4); but should you do what is wrong, you may well be afraid, for that sword is no empty badge because the law officer becomes a servant of God to bring punishment to those who practice evil! It is therefore necessary to submit both for fear of punishment and "because of conscience" (13:5). The Christian cannot afford to do wrong, not just because of the long arm of the state to administer punishment, but also because from the heart he has the desire to do what is right, not only in duties to God, but also in duties to society and its members.

Can Government Get Out of Order?

It should be noted that Romans 13 does not take up the issue of how to behave when the state steps out of its bounds and attempts to suppress the proclamation of the gospel, as, for example, when the Jewish Sanhedrin tried to tell the apostles to stop teaching about Jesus. The apostles vigorously rejected that kind of an improper demand (Acts 4:18-20). Then, and then only, is it right before God to tell the state in no uncertain terms that Christians have no alternative but to "obey God rather than men!" (Acts 5:29). And this every Christian must do!

"This is also why you pay taxes" (13:6). Taxes serve to bear the cost of operating the government. The non-Christian in some cases may pay because the government has the power to collect taxes, but the Christian, recognizing that it is God's will for secular government to function, pays also for conscience' sake. (The Swiss Brethren paid all taxes, following this instruction. But the Hutterites refused to pay special war taxes.) In this case Paul uses a different word for servants; the word can be used of priests, although as the Arndt-Gingrich *Greek Lexicon* points out (p. 472), it is here used "of pagan government officials." Note also the word of Christ on this subject (Matthew 22; Mark 12; Luke 20). Give everyone what they are entitled to, says Paul, whether taxes, revenue, respect, or honor (13:7).

What about the teaching of Revelation 13? Is the instruction there different from that of Romans 13? Revelation 13 portrays a persecuting government, not merely one looking after the general welfare. Although Revelation speaks of a persectuion unto death, there is not a syllable there calling for anything but "patient endurance" and for "faithfulness" (Revelation 13:10)—this in spite of most trying circumstances. The Christian under every kind of situation is to be submissive to the government. But the Christian must reserve the right to "obey God rather than men" should a conflict with God's holy law occur. This includes all taking of human life, any support of social injustice, and other sin.

The Primacy of Love: 13:8-10

Stay out of debt, says the apostle, except the debt to live by love. For it is he who lives by love who keeps the entire law—all the commandments such as not to commit adultery, not to kill people, not to steal, and not to have evil desire. "Love does no harm to its neighbor. Therefore love is the fulfillment of the law" (13:10). A full and thorough study of what leads to complete happiness both here and hereafter leads to the vindication of the law of God. Living totally by love leads to full conformity to the law of God.

Hope that Sanctifies: 13:11-14

Paul looks upon the bride of Christ, the church, as living in the hope of the bridegroom's return. And having this hope of Christ's coming does something to people. There is no place in the Christian life for carelessness, for spiritual drowsiness. The apostle urges his readers, "It is time to wake up . . . because our salvation is nearer than when we first believed. The night is clearly over; the day [of Christ's return] is almost here." This awareness is a clear call to holy living; it should also exclude any disunity in the church. Christians shall live in holiness, not even giving thought to gratifying the lusts of the flesh. And there is only one way to be spiritually safe; that is to "clothe [ourselves] . . . with the Lord Jesus Christ" (13:14).

10

Bring ideal scripture that stood out.

The Considerate Church Member

(Romans 14—16)

The Considerate Church Member: 14:1—15:22

Human nature is no different now from Paul's day. People have always tended to look at issues in terms of their own experience. Each person sees the issues before him through his own glasses. Equally sincere people differ on minor matters. In the two chapters before us Paul takes up three issues with the potential for disunity among and tension between sincere believers.

First, he says we do not need to ask for absolute maturity on the part of those who enter the church. Then he asks, what about the vegetarian? (14:2). Paul makes it clear what the Christian position is: There is no good reason why eating meat should be a handicap to a believer. Now it is obvious that although Christianity involves the total person, one is not a Christian either by eating meat or by not eating it. It is simply a matter of personal preference; that is, to one who is "mature," such as the apostle. There is always the possibility that a given advocate of an abstemious program will magnify his scruples into a much larger issue than others do.

Paul cautions both the eater and the non-eater of meat. He tells the meat-eater not to look down on or despise the

130

vegetarian; and immediately he turns around and urges the vegetarian not to pass judgment on the one who eats both meat and vegetables. The important thing is not one's diet: it is rather a matter of having faith in Christ. And regardless of diet, God fully accepts every believer. Who are we to judge the servant of someone else? "To his own master he stands or falls" (14:4). And then Paul brings his robust faith to play on the issue before him: "He will stand, for the Lord is able to make him stand" (14:4)!

What about the Sabbatarian? (14:5). The first case Paul discussed had to do with scruples about food. Now we come to a person whose scruples had to do with holy days. The problem was probably most acute for those of Jewish background. The Jews had a weekly holy day (the Sabbath), a monthly holy day (the New Moon), and an annual holy day (The Day of Atonement), in addition to the several festivals. Ought Jewish Christians, in particular, show special reverence for certain days in the Jewish calendar? In Galatia, where a full-blown Judaizing school was active, Paul sharply criticized all forms of Judaism which were slipping into accepted Christian practice. (See especially Galatians 4:10: "You are observing special days and months and seasons and years!" and Colossians 2:16: "Therefore do not let anyone judge you by what you eat or drink, or with regard to a religious festival [annual], a New Moon celebration [monthly] or a Sabbath day [weekly]."

Can devout Jews be blamed for wanting to cling to circumcision and to their holy days? Take the institution of the Sabbath, for example. Exodus 31:13 says that the keeping of Israel's Sabbaths was a sign between Jahweh, Israel's covenant God, and his people Israel "for the generations to come," and "as a lasting covenant" (31:16). Similar language is used of the covenant of circumcision in Genesis 17. Yet the same sovereign God who gave these symbols was above his own regulations and could declare them to be ended in their old form by Christ and his cross.

Actually, the most surprising factor here is the sharpness with which Paul attacks the Judaizing confusion in Galatians (about AD 57) and Colossians (about AD 62), while taking a rather bland and mild stance in Romans (about AD 58). Here he seems to say, "Let everyone select the view with which he agrees and at the same time hold in warm love the brother or sister who takes a different view." The apparent contradiction is, however, not real. Paul wrote Galatians and even Colossians to churches where he felt the truth of the gospel was at stake. Here it was more a matter of different Christians holding to differing views without seriously threatening the unity of the believers. Here the big concern of the apostle was to help all the members of the church to be accepting and considerate—not to pass judgment on one another nor to look down on those who differ. Just leave the judging to God since he will be the ultimate Judge anyhow! As usual, he buttresses his point with a word from Isaiah 49:18 and 45:23 (Romans 14:11), pointing out that "each of us will [have to] give an account of himself to God" (14:12).

Don't Live to Please Self

We must stop living just for ourselves, pleads Paul. We must at every point take into account the other members of Christ's body. Most of all, we must avoid putting a stumbling block in front of a brother or sister to stumble over, so that his or her faith is shaken. Also, says Paul, it is clear that to violate one's own scruples, to do what one feels is wrong, is itself a sin (whether the act in itself is intrinsically wrong or not): "If anyone regards something as unclean, then for him it is unclean" (14:14). Then comes the most solemn appeal of all: "Do not ... destroy your brother for whom Christ died" (14:15)! It would be an awful tragedy if you flaunted your Christian liberty in a manner to confuse a weaker brother. He trusts you, and therefore feels: "If he can eat foods, surely I can too!" Actually, however, because he does not feel free to eat what you can eat with a clear conscience, in his confusion he eats also, and then suffers from having violated his conscience. Paul even suggests that the erring brother might go on from one sin to another, until he is apostate! Don't do it, cries Paul; do not ruin your weak brother! It is love, agape love, which limits our freedom in Christ. The Spirit-led Christian will pray for daily guidance that he may know in what areas he is free to act without anxiety, and in which ones to be more cautious and considerate.

What Is Involved in Membership in the Kingdom of God?

It is not a matter of eating and drinking, says Paul, but "righteousness, peace and joy in the Holy Spirit" (14:17). He who is so yielded to the Spirit of God that these three nouns describe him may rest assured that he is both, "pleasing to God and approved by men" [anthropois] or people (14:18). The two keys are (1) "what leads to peace;" and (2) what enhances "mutual edification" (14:19). "Do not destroy the work of God for the sake of food" (14:20) is a powerful plea for the immeasurably greater significance of God's work among people than of an individual's preferences for specific foods.

In Romans 14:14 the brother with a weak conscience is urged not to damage himself spiritually by violating his conscience. Now in 14:20 the brother with no special scruples about foods is told plainly that "it is wrong for a man [anthropos] to eat anything that causes someone else to stumble." Love modifies Christian freedom. This applies to eating meat, to drinking wine, and to anything else which could cause your brother to fall (14:21). A good rule for oneself is to do only what one can do with a clear conscience, what one can do from a stance of faith in Christ (14:22).

It is really a basic principle not to live for our own pleasure (15:1-3). Christ is a perfect example of this principle of living for the welfare of others. If he had lived for himself, he would certainly not have set his face steadfastly to go up to Jerusalem. He would not have yielded to the will of his heavenly Father in the Garden of Gethsemane. Much less would he have meekly allowed himself to be crucified as a felon!

Paul's most fundamental concern, as he struggles with these questions of conscience, is that the members of the church at Rome might receive from God himself the gifts of *endurance* and of *encouragement,* and that they might have a *spirit of unity* among themselves as they *follow Christ Jesus.* This will enable them "with one heart and mouth [to] ... glorify the God and Father of our Lord Jesus Christ" (15:6).

What About the Jewish Racist?

The greatest threat to unity in the apostolic church was surely the cleavage between the Jews and Gentiles. Therefore Paul reminded the Jews that Christ has become a servant or minister (diakonos) to the Jews "to confirm the promises made to the patriarchs," Abraham, Isaac, and Jacob (15:8). Exultantly, he quotes one Old Testament prophecy after another to show the joyous welcome God has for believing Gentiles who also come to faith in Israel's Messiah and are thus made into one undivided unity in the Lord Jesus. Paul indicates clearly that it is his task, his *priestly duty,* to proclaim the gospel to the Gentiles so that they "might become an offering acceptable to God [having been] sanctified by the Holy Spirit" (15:16). Paul recognizes the source of his power to win Gentiles: it was Christ himself who had used Paul to lead "the Gentiles to obey God" (15:18). Christ had empowered Paul with "signs and miracles, [and granted him] ... the power of the [Holy] Spirit" (15:19; cf. 2 Corinthians 12:12). Then, with a vast thousand-mile sweep, Paul indicates that he had fully proclaimed the gospel of Christ, establishing a chain of Christian congregations across the Roman Empire, even where Christ was not known, for it was Paul's joy to lay the foundation of Christian faith (15:20). Perhaps it was because Paul was so busily engaged in establishing Gentile congregations in the Roman Empire that he was so frequently hindered in going to Rome (15:22).

Epilogue: Travel Plans, Warnings, Greetings, Blessing, Doxology: 15:23—16:27 Rome and Spain: 15:23-33

Now at last the time seems to be coming for Paul to go to Spain, a trip he had desired to take for a long time. At the moment, however, Paul had a quite different mission to fulfill. There were many poor and needy believers in the church at Jerusalem, which would have been justified in calling itself the "mother church." It was at Jerusalem that our Lord was crucified and God raised him from the dead, and it was there that the Christian church was actually established when the enthroned Messiah, the glorified Christ Jesus, poured out his blessed Spirit on Pentecost.

When the Gentile churches in the provinces of Macedonia and Achaia learned of the need of the brothers and sisters at Jerusalem, they joyously raised funds to aid the Jerusalem church. Paul says "they were *pleased to do it*" (15:27) and he added that it was also their obligation, an obligation of love, of course. It was an exchange of gifts: On the one hand, the Jews shared, so to speak, their Messiah with the Gentiles, for when the Gentiles were converted and became believers on the Lord Jesus, it was clear to everyone that the church was now partly Jewish and partly Gentile, yet it was united in one body of faith and love. On the other hand, says Paul, if the Jews shared their spiritual blessings with the Gentiles, then the Gentiles also have an obligation to share their material blessings with the Jews in need (15:27). Then as soon as Paul has completed his ministry to his people, he hopes to come to Rome, and he is confident that he "will come in the full measure of the blessing of Christ" (15:29).

Pray for Me!

This is no stereotyped request. It is clear that Paul feels the need of prayer. He appeals to them in the name of Christ, "and by the love of the Spirit, to join" (15:30) him in prayer, to "co-agonize" with him, beseeching God to rescue him from the unbelievers in Judea and to make his ministry to the saints in Jerusalem acceptable. Then, he continues, "I [will] . . . come to you with joy" (15:32), and stop off at Rome on his way to Spain. . . .

Little did Paul know at this point of all the setbacks he would experience in Jerusalem: arrest, rescue by the Roman soldiers, appearance before the Sanhedrin (Council or Parliament) of the Jews, escape from a plot of over forty men to kill him, a military escort to Caesarea, two years of prison there, and finally the famous shipwreck journey to Rome as a prisoner of the Romans. Nor does Acts reveal anything of the years of Paul after AD 63. The only clues we have are in the so-called pastoral epistles where Paul's circumstances and attitudes are altogether different from those in his first Roman imprisonment when he wrote Colossians, Philemon, Ephesians, and Philippians.

Welcome Phoebe

When Paul wrote Romans he was in Corinth, and Corinth had a seaport called Cenchreae. The port included a town with a Christian church. One of the members at Cenchreae was a woman named Phoebe. She was a servant like her Lord, who was also called a servant (diakonos)—as were Paul and many other members. Phoebe was known for the way she practiced servanthood among the brothers and sisters. Indeed, the church at Cenchreae may have commissioned Phoebe to do the work among the sisters especially, which the male deacons may have been assigned to, for she is called by the very same Greek term which was given the deacons in Philippians 1:1 and in 1 Timothy 3:8-13. The Arndt-Gingrich *Greek Lexicon* defines the Greek word generally as "servant" or "helper," then specifically as "deacon" (a church official), and finally as "deaconess," citing Romans 16:1. Other scholars, however, take the word to mean a servant generally. It is often assumed that Phoebe carried the epistle of Paul to the Roman church. In any case Paul commends her highly—"for she has been a great help to many people, including me" (16:2).

Greetings

The first people Paul greeted in the Roman church were Priscilla and Aquila (Acts 18:2) who "risked their lives for me" (16:4).

Meetinghouses (special buildings for congregations to worship in) were not constructed for a couple centuries after Paul wrote Romans. But he does mention a number of house churches, such as the congregation which met in the house of Aquila and Priscilla, Paul's co-workers (16:5). Note the way Paul recognizes the great role played by Christian women in the work of the church.

Paul hurries on to the first Christian convert he had in Asia, a man named Epenetus; then a woman named Mary, who worked hard for the church at Rome. Special greetings to his relatives follow, Andronicus and Junias, who had been imprisoned with Paul. Greetings follow rapidly for Ampliatus, Urbanus, Stachys, Apelles, the household of Aristobulus, Herodion, the household of Narcissus, Tryphena and Tryphosa, Persis, Rufus and his mother, Asyncritus, Phlegon, Hermes, Patrobas, Hermas and the brothers with him, Philologus, Julia, Nereus and his sister, and Olympas, and all the saints with them. Travel was rather easy in those days, and many people found their way to Rome.

As in a number of other epistles, Paul urges the use of the holy kiss as a warm Christian greeting (16:16). He also passed on greetings from all the churches of Christ.

Avoid Schismatics

Paul had spent considerable energy trying to get potential factions in the church at Rome to relate to the rest of the body in a loving and accepting manner. Paul saw no justification for splitting the church in any conceivable way. The unity of the body is the concern of the Holy Spirit, and it was Paul's concern as well. Carnality leads to schisms, but the Holy Spirit leads to penitence, renewal, and unity. He therefore uses such phrases as "watch out for those who cause divisions"; "keep away from them" (16:17). They are utterly selfish! They deceive people! Paul is wholly critical of people who split congregations. They are following the flesh, not the Spirit of God.

Imminent Victory

"The God of peace will soon crush Satan under your feet"

(16:20). Paul is confident that the resources for victory, total victory, are available to the brothers and sisters at Rome, and they will soon claim that victory! We do not know, and we need not know, what all the trials and temptations were. But we do know who is bound to come out on top if the resources of God's Spirit are utilized! It is God who is sovereign.

Blessing

"The grace of our Lord Jesus be with you" (16:20). May you experience, says the apostle, the pure gift of God, his total favor, through the crucified, resurrected, ascended, enthroned, and interceding Savior. May you have total well-being, Hebrew *shalom,* through your faith union with Christ.

Other Greetings

Perhaps because he was Paul's most trusted disciple and colleague, Paul was indeed happy to convey the personal greetings of his beloved Timothy to the church in Rome. Also sending greetings were relatives of Paul: Lucius, Jason, and Sosipater. Then there are greetings also from Tertius, Paul's secretary who wrote the letter at Paul's dictation; the hospitable Gaius of Corinth; a Christian named Quartus; and finally the most auspicious of all, Erastus. Paul calls him the steward or manager of the city; most modern versions seem to favor "city treasurer." But about thirty years ago an archaeologist who was working in ancient Corinth made a discovery which might refer to this Erastus and which could throw light on his position. A paving block contains an inscription indicating that Erastus had borne the expense of the paving, and that he held the position which might be translated as Commissioner of Public Works, a reading which was basically adopted by the NIV: "the city's director of public works" (16:23). (Everett F. Harrison. *Romans,* p. 169. In Frank E. Gaebelein. *The Expositor's Bible Commentary.* Grand Rapids, Michigan: Zondervan Publishing House, 1976.)

A Beautiful Doxology

"Now to him who is able to establish you by my gospel and

the proclamation of Jesus Christ, according to the revelation of the mystery hidden for long ages past, but now revealed and made known through the prophetic writings by the command of the eternal God, so that all nations might believe and obey him—to the only wise God be glory forever through Jesus Christ! Amen" (16:25-27).

Appendix

Menno Speaks

Menno Simons (c. 1496-1561), after whom the Mennonite Church is named, has much to say which is relevant to Paul's letter to the Romans. What follows are quotes from Menno keyed to each of the chapters of this commentary on Romans. The quotes are from *The Complete Writings of Menno Simons,* Translated from the Dutch by Leonard Verduin and edited by J. C. Wenger, with a biography by Harold S. Bender (Scottdale, Pa.), 1956.

Chapter 1: *All People Need Deliverance*

On the corruption of human nature by sin and depravity:

"... Although Christ, the Prince of our salvation, has led us to His glory and accepted us as brethren and children in faith, yet we are in our first birth derived from Adam and so poisoned by the serpent and so corrupted by nature, that we can nevermore become free of our unclean flesh so long as we dwell in this tabernacle; but ofttimes (although against our will) mix and soil ourselves therewith and become convinced ... that according to the eternal justice we are guilty of death" (p. 827).

"Behold, precious reader, if you would rightly know and acknowledge how miserable, naked, powerless, impotent, unclean, sinful, and poisoned all of Adam's seed is become in him, through his transgression, and how his seed is ... fallen into his wrath, judgment,

140

curse, condemnation and death, then, I say, Search the Law diligently. For it points out to you, first, the obedience to God and righteousness required of you; and also the weakness of your sinful flesh, your impure and evil-disposed nature; and that you are already condemned to death ... since you, through your inherent weak nature and evil-disposed flesh, do not walk in the required righteousness as God has commanded and required of you in His Law. The anointing that is with you, if you will only observe it, will make it plain" (p. 818).

Chapter 2: *The Good News: Righteousness by Faith*

On Depravity: "But as to my poor, weak, and imperfect life, I freely confess that I am a poor, miserable sinner, conceived in sin, of sinful seed, and sinfully brought forth. I can say with David that my sins are ever before me. My thoughts, words, and actions convict me. With the holy Paul I observe that in me, that is, in my flesh, dwelleth no good thing. (p. 673).

"If God should judge us according to our deserts, and not according to His great goodness and mercy ... no man could stand before His judgment.... Therefore it should be far from us that we should comfort ourselves with anything but the grace of God through Christ Jesus. For He it is and He alone and none other who has perfectly fulfilled the righteousness required by God....

"For Christ's sake we are in grace; for His sake we are heard; and for His sake our faults and failings which are committed against our will are remitted. For it is He who stands between His Father and His imperfect children, with His perfect righteousness.... We are to be saved solely by grace through Christ Jesus.... In short, by grace eternal life is given us through Christ Jesus" (pp. 506-507).

"All false doctrine tends to deny the true mercy seat, Jesus Christ, who alone is our righteousness...." (p. 157).

Chapter 3. *Abraham, Father of Believers*

On our innate perversity, Menno is frankly autobiographical:

"O Lord of hosts, when I am buoyed up in the waters of Thy grace, I find that I can neither fathom nor measure them.... Who, dear Lord, ever came to Thee with a pious heart and was rejected? Who ever sought Thee and found Thee not?... Yes, dear Lord, how many didst Thou accept in grace who otherwise by Thy stern justice merited otherwise?...

"I also, dear Lord, the greatest of all sinners, and the least among all the saints, am not worthy to be called Thy child or servant, for I have sinned against heaven and before Thee. Although I resisted in former times Thy precious Word and Thy holy will with all my powers, and with full understanding contended against Thy manifest truth, taught and lived and sought my own flesh, praise, and honor, more than Thy righteousness, honor, word, and truth; nevertheless Thy fatherly grace did not forsake me, a miserable sinner, but in love received me, converted me to another mind, led me with the right hand, and taught me by the Holy Spirit until of my own choice I declared war upon the world, the flesh, and the devil ... I repeat, Thy mercies are greater than all Thy works...." (p. 69).

"You see, kind reader, we do not seek our salvation in works, words, or sacraments as do the learned ones [the state church clergy], although they accuse us of that very thing, but we seek them only in Christ Jesus and in no other means in heaven or on earth....

"All those who accept this proffered means of divine grace, Jesus Christ, with believing hearts, enclose Him in the treasure box of their minds. They believe and confess that their sins are forgiven for the sake of His sacrifice, death and blood; that nevermore His wrath and damnation will be upon them; that He accepts them as His dear sons and daughters, and gives them eternal life. All such become joyous and glad in the Spirit, and give thanks to God with renewed hearts, for the power of faith quickens and changes them into newness of life, and they walk by the gift of grace in the Holy Spirit in the power of their new faith..." (p. 505).

Chapter 4: *The Fruit of Faith in Christ*

On the nature of faith in Christ:

"True faith ... is the mother which bears all Christian virtues, and by reason of this, the Word of God ascribes everything to it, such as righteousness (Romans 3:23 and 5:1), blessing (Galatians 3:14), salvation (Mark 16:16), and life everlasting (John 3:36; 17:4). It does not ascribe these to ceremonies, but it is because of the faith which compels us to observe these ceremonies, since they are commanded of God. Therefore know, kind reader, that when the ceremonies in God's Word are coupled with the promise, as the Israelitish sacrifices in the Law, and baptism under the Gospel, then it is not because of ceremony but it is by virtue of faith, which obediently and in love fulfills not only the commanded ceremonies, but also all that which God has commanded ..." (p. 267).

"We cannot obtain salvation, grace, reconciliation, nor peace of the Father otherwise than through Christ Jesus. As He Himself says, No man cometh unto the Father but by me. Peter also says, There is none other name under heaven given among men, whereby we must be saved, than the name of Jesus; and that all those who accept this grace in Christ, preached by the Gospel and accepted by a firm faith, and cordially adhered to by power of the Holy Spirit through faith, become new men born of God. Such men are changed in their hearts, renewed and of a different mind; yes, transferred from Adam unto Christ ..." (p. 507).

"The Scriptures teach plainly that we have all become sinners in Adam, and that we have all fallen under the judgment, wrath, and condemnation of God, through sin, and become subject unto death ..." (p. 805).

"It is a very precious word which Paul speaks, When we were yet without strength, in due time Christ died for the ungodly. Yea, when we were yet ungodly, and thereby He manifests His love toward us. For if, when we were enemies, we were reconciled to God by the death of His Son, much more, being reconciled, we shall be saved by His life ..." (p. 1053).

"The Scriptures as I see it speak of different kinds of sin. The first kind is the corrupt, sinful nature, namely, the lust or desire of our flesh contrary to God's Law ... sin which is inherited at birth by all descendants and children of corrupt, sinful Adam, and is not inaptly called original sin.... Paul says, We were by nature children of wrath, even as others.

"Yes, readers, since we all partake of this evil, therefore we would have all continued in death if the righteousness, intercession, death, and blood of Christ Jesus were not given us as a reconciliation to God.... But now for Christ's sake, it is not counted as sin unto us....

"The second kind of sins are the fruits of this first sin and are not inaptly called actual sins by theologians.... These are also called works of the flesh by Paul ... and that because they have their origin in the flesh which is born of Adam, corrupt and sinful....

"The third kind of sins are human frailties, errors, and stumblings which are still found daily among saints and regenerate ones.... The unbelieving ones ... commit sin with relish and boldness.... But those who are born from above are fearful of all sin.... They fight daily with it inward or outward, important or trifling....

"The fourth kind of sin is [the wicked blasphemy against the Holy Spirit, ascribing His blessed work to the devil, the end of which state is death]" (p. 563-565).

"We confess that even as the Almighty, eternal Father through mere grace and love has in the beginning created Adam and Eve by Christ ... now that they together with their entire seed have fallen, has by the same Word ... raised them up again out of pure grace and love, accepted them as His children ... through the Word or Son ..." (p. 885).

"... Paul writes, He ... spared not His own Son.... Also this, We are reconciled to God by the death of His Son.... At another place, God sent His Son to be the mercy seat or propitiation for our sins ..." (p. 904).

"He was like unto us in all things, sin excepted.... All who believe on Him have through Him received grace, mercy, forgiveness of sins, and eternal life, and that by means of His crimson blood which He has in His great love sacrificed and shed on the cross for us poor sinners, according to the good pleasure of the Father. And so He has become our only and eternal High Priest, Atoner, Mercy Seat, Mediator, and Advocate with God His Father" (pp. 492-493).

"These are they who are justified by faith and have peace with God, through our Lord Jesus Christ, by whom also we have access by faith into this grace wherein we stand, and rejoice in hope of the glory of God ...

"There is none that can glory in himself touching this faith, for it is the gift of God.... Happy is he to whom God gives this gift.... He that receives it receives Christ Jesus, forgiveness of sins, a new mind, and eternal life. For true faith which is acceptable before God cannot be barren; it mus bring forth fruit and manifest its nature. It works ceaselessly in love, enters willingly into righteousness, mortifies flesh and blood, crucifies the lusts and desires, rejoices in the cross of Christ, renews and regenerates. It makes one active, confident, and joyful in Christ Jesus. Such a faith, I say, is the gift of God ..." (p. 116).

"We are all created in Adam ... and have become of a sinful nature and subject to death.... We also ... are graciously accepted of

God [through Christ] and mercifully called unto life everlasting
[Romans 5:12 and John 3:16]" (p. 800).

"He graciously fulfilled the spiritual law . . . in perfect righteousness, trod the winepress of bitter wrath for us. . . . He has all power in
heaven and upon earth, and is through the sacrifice of His death and
blood our only and eternal mercy seat, Reconciler, High Priest, Mediator, Advocate, and Peacemaker with God His Father" (p. 909).

"It was as if He wanted to say: Behold, dear children, so far has
that love which I have had for you and the whole human race
constrained me, and ever shall, that I left the glory of my Father, and
came into this sad world as a poor slave to serve you. For I saw that
you all belonged to the devil, and that there was none to redeem you;
that you had all gone astray like erring sheep, and there was none who
cared for you; that you were a prey to devouring wolves, and there was
none to save you; that you were wounded unto death, and' there was
none that could heal you. Therefore did I come from heaven, and became a poor, weak, and dying man, in all things like unto you, sin excepted. In my great love I sought you out with zeal, found you
miserable, sorrowful, yes, half dead. The services of my love I have
demonstrated so heartily toward you; your sores I bandaged; your
blood I wiped away; wine and oil I have poured into your putrid
wounds; set you free from the jaws of the hellish beasts; I took you
upon my shoulders and led you into the tabernacles of peace. Your
nakedness I covered; I had compassion on your misery; the law I have
fulfilled for you; your sins I took away. The peace, grace, and favor of
my Father I proclaimed to you; His good will I revealed; the way of
truth I pointed out; and I have powerfully testified to you by my marvelous signs and great miracles that I am the true Messiah, the
promised Prince and Savior" (p. 147).

Chapter 5: *The Believer Delivered*

What it means to be in Christ:

"The holy Paul teaches us saying, For we are all children of God
by faith in Christ Jesus. For as many of you as have been baptized into
Christ, have put on Christ" (p. 267).

"[Those who are in Christ] fight daily with their weak flesh in the
Spirit and in faith. They sigh and lament about their errors. . . . They
are not rejected by the Lord on account of such lapses. . . . The seed of

God, faith in Christ Jesus, the birth which is of God, and the anointing of the Holy Spirit, remain in them ... and although they are such poor, imperfect children, they nevertheless rejoice in the sure trust of the merits of Christ, and praise the Father for His grace" (p. 564).

"Therefore I admonish all our beloved brethren and sisters in the Lord ... never to forget to what you were called, taught, and baptized. Remember the covenant of the Most High which you voluntarily desired and accepted, being taught by the Word of God, and led by the Holy Spirit. Remember that according to the doctrine of Paul, you have voluntarily buried in baptism all your avarice, uncleanness, pride, hatred, envy, abuse of the sacramental signs, idolatry, gluttony, drunkenness, sensuality, falsehood, deceit, etc., and that you are arisen with Christ Jesus into newness of life (Romans 6), if so be you are truly risen with Him. This new life is nothing but righteousness, unblamableness, love, mercy, humility, long-suffering, peace, truth; yes, the whole gentle life which is taught by the gospel and experienced in Christ Jesus.

"O brethren, how far some of us, alas, are still distant from the evangelical life which is of God! Notwithstanding that they stay out of the [state] churches and are outwardly baptized with water, yet they are earthly and carnally minded in all things, thinking perhaps that Christianity consists in external baptism and staying away from the [state] churches. Oh dear, No! I tell you as truly as the Lord lives, before God no outward baptism counts, nor staying away from the churches, nor Lord's Supper, nor persecution, if there is no obedience to the commandments of God, and no faith which manifests itself in love, and no new creature.... Except a man be born again, he cannot see the kingdom of God.... Except ye become as little children, ye shall not enter the kingdom of heaven. But the regenerated bury their sins in baptism and arise with Christ into newness of life (Romans 6)" (pp. 410-411; cf. pp. 122, 267, 239, 513, 885).

"For we are not regenerated because we are baptized ... but we are baptized because we are regenerated ... " (pp. 264-265).

"Know that we are not accepted into the covenant by an outward sign, but only through Christ Jesus" (p. 262).

"We do not seek our salvation in works, words, or sacraments ... but we seek them only in Christ Jesus.... We rejoice exclusively in this only means....

"But that we abhor carnal works, and desire to conform ourselves to His Word and commandment, according to our weakness, we do because He so taught and commanded us. For whosoever does not walk according to His doctrine, proves in fact that he does not believe on Him or know Him and that he is not in the communion of the saints" (pp. 504-505).

"I am heartily sorry that I fail to walk in Christ with all my strength according to God's will, and be a righteous and blameless Christian; and that I am unable to beget the whole world out of its proud and godless life, unto a new and penitent Christian life.... For my only joy and my heart's desire is that we might rightly preach Christ, according to His holy Word, magnify His holy name, seek Him, fear Him, love Him, and serve Him; yes, that we might be the city of the living God, the glorious kingdom of His honor, and the temple of His Holy Spirit ... " (p. 791).

On the spiritual status of children:

"To children belongs the kingdom of God, not by virtue of any sign, but by grace alone through Christ Jesus" (p. 685).

"But little children and particularly those of Christian parentage have a peculiar promise which was given them of God without any ceremony, but out of pure and generous grace, through Christ Jesus our Lord, who says, Suffer little children and forbid them not, to come unto me; for of such is the kingdom of heaven. Matthew 19:14; Mark 10:14; Luke 18:16. This promise makes glad and assures all the chosen saints of God in regard to their children or infants. By it they are assured that the true word of our beloved Lord Jesus Christ could never fail. Inasmuch as He has shown such great mercy toward the children that were brought to Him that He took them up in His blessed arms, blessed them, laid His hands upon them, promised them the kingdom of heaven, and has done no more with them; therefore such parents have in their hearts a sure and firm faith in the grace of God concerning their beloved children, namely that they are children of the kingdom, of grace, and of the promise of eternal life through Jesus Christ our Lord, to whom alone be the glory, and not by any ceremony. Yes, by such promise they were assured that their dear children, as long as they are mere children, are clean, holy, saved, and pleasing unto God, be they alive or dead. Therefore they give thanks to the eternal Father through Jesus Christ our Lord for His inexpressibly great love to their dear children, and they train them in the love of God and in wisdom by correcting, chastising, teaching, and admonishing them, and by the example of an irreproachable life, until these children are able to hear the Word of God, to believe it, and to fulfill it in their works. Then is the time and not until then, of whatever age they may be, that they should receive Christian baptism, which Christ Jesus has commanded in obedience to His Word to all Christians, and which His apostles have practiced and taught" (pp. 280-281).

"Little ones must wait according to God's Word until they can understand the holy Gospel of Grace and sincerely confess it; and then, and then only is it time, no matter how young or how old, for them to receive Christian baptism as the infallible Word of our beloved Lord Jesus Christ has taught and commanded all true believers in His holy Gospel. . . . If they die before coming to years of discretion, that is, in childhood, before they come to years of understanding and before they have faith, then they die under the promise of God, and that by no other means than the generous promise of grace given through Christ Jesus" (p. 241).

"As often as we are asked why infants are not to be baptized, since they are in the church of God, in grace, in covenant, in promise, we answer, Because the Lord neither taught nor commanded it" (p. 136; cf. pp. 698, 708).

Chapter 6: *Liberation, Not Perfectionism*

In commenting on Hebrews 2:14-17, ("Since the children partake of flesh and blood"), Menno writes:

"First, observe that the word *children* has reference to none other than those who are called Christ's brethren earlier, namely, those who believe in Him, and who are born of God by the living power of His Spirit and Word. . . .

"Second, observe that the scriptural meaning of *having communion with* [in Menno's Bible read thus for *partake of*] *flesh and blood* is not simply having flesh and blood . . . but it also means to be intimate with flesh and blood, and do things which are forbidden of God, through the lusts of our flesh.

"Third, observe that since the said children still have fellowship with sinful flesh and blood and are still subject to such human weakness (although contrary to their will) by which they continually fall and fail, therefore they must have such a High Priest who could have compassion with their human failures, since He was tempted in the same manner, although without sin . . . " (pp. 823-824).

Since Hebrews 2:16 indicates that Christ did not take on the nature of angels, but the seed of Abraham, Menno writes: ". . . He takes on Him the seed of Abraham, the children of promise (Romans 9:8); the believers (Galatians 3:29); His brethren and children. He accepts them in grace to the praise of His Father (Romans 15:7); prays for their faults and weaknesses. Romans 8:7; Hebrews 5:10. For they can never be freed from the inherent, impure, wicked nature of their sinful flesh in this life" (p. 827).

Against the charge of perfectionism, he wrote: "Do receive my admonishing confession in good nature, and do not think it is too strict, namely, such words as clean, unblamable, and the like. For they are spoken of Christ Jesus Himself, and of His holy apostles to the church of the Lord. John 13:10; Philippians 2:15. Do not understand, most beloved, that we deem ourselves so clean and unblamable as to be without sin. No, not at all, dear brethren, for I know full well that the holy John teaches, saying, If we say that we have no sin, we deceive ourselves, and the truth is not in us. 1 John 1:8. For as James says, In many things we all offend. James 3:2. Yes, dear brethren, with Paul I find the appetite to commit sin so strong in my flesh at all times that I often think recklessly, speak rashly, and do the evil which I would not.

"But the abominable, shameful sins and offenses, such as adultery, fornication, hatred, envy, drunkenness, pomp, splendor, cursing, swearing, gambling, desire of filthy lucre, abuse of the ordinances of Christ, and lying and fraud, I verily detest from the bottom of my heart. And they should never, by the grace of the Lord, be practiced by any sincere, God-fearing Christians, inasmuch as they hate and oppose them. For the Spirit which is in true Christians is a deadly enemy to all wickedness and sin (at the same time we often find that we are born of Adam). And their spirit strives and hungers after the truth, righteousness, will, and commandment of God—yet in great weakness; for they are very much retarded in the works, fruits, and fulfillment by the heavy burden of the sinful flesh. Nevertheless, because the good Spirit of God abides in them, they do not cease to fight against their flesh, so often their hindrance. For the life of true Christians is nothing but an endless struggle upon earth. Whosoever shall fight valiantly and overcome, he will be clothed in white raiment and will be fed with the heavenly bread of the tree of life. Revelation 2:17; 3:5" (p. 447).

"The reason they throw the ugly word of hypocrite at us and lyingly say that we boast of being without sin is because we teach penitence according to the Scriptures, because we testify with the holy Paul that adulterers, idolaters, drunkards, avaricious, liars, and the unrighteous shall not inherit the kingdom of God; that those who are carnally minded shall die; and with John that those who sin willfully and of set purpose are of the devil, and that we therefore even in our weakness have an aversion to such works, although with Moses we have often confessed with tongue and pen, and ever will confess that none is clear before God because of innate sin. We say with Isaiah that we are all as the unclean; with David, that there is no living man righteous before God; with Paul, that nothing good dwells in our flesh; with John, that if we say that we are without sin we deceive ourselves and no truth is in us; and with James, that in many things we all offend" (p. 568).

"We confess and say, and that in accordance with our Lord's Word, that the Scripture exempts none from sin but Him that is free indeed, namely, Christ Jesus (Isaiah 53:12). . . .

"We say that it is the doctrine of the holy Scripture that none born of the guilty and sinful flesh of Adam could fulfill the law which was spiritual; for the seed of Adam was too much corrupted; and was also by the righteous judgment of God subject to the curse. Deuteronomy 27:26. Inasmuch then as it became altogether helpless and weak in Adam, and the law continues to accuse us before God, therefore He in His great love took pity on Adam and all his seed and did not spare His own Son, but sent Him in the form of sinful flesh. Romans 8:3, 32. He fulfilled the law for us, who without guilt Himself died for us guilty sinners that through Him we might live. And so He became our holy, innocent, and spotless High Priest, Mediator, Advocate, and Reconciler with God His Father . . . (p. 870).

Chapter 7: *The Spirit-filled Life*

On the Christian life:

". . . A genuine Christian faith cannot lie idle, but it changes, renews, purifies, sanctifies, and justifies more and more. It gives peace and joy, for by faith it knows that hell, the devil, sin, and death are conquered through Christ, and that grace, mercy, pardon from sin, and eternal life are acquired through Him. In full confidence it approaches the Father in the name of Christ, receives the Holy Ghost, becomes partaker of the divine nature, and is renewed after the image of Him who created him. It lives out of the power of Christ which is in it; all its ways are righteousness, godliness, honesty, chastity, truth, wisdom, goodness, kindliness, light, love, peace (p. 396).

"Since we are entangled by such wicked, sinful, disobedient, and guilty flesh . . . [Christ] has come boldly forward to battle for His subjects, His sanctified brethren and children. He . . . has vanquished [the tempter] in his power; has taken his weapons, bruised his head, satisfied and blotted out the handwriting; erased it with His crimson blood; discharged our guilty and deserved death by his innocent and undeserved death to the fulfillment of the prophetic word . . . He has thus delivered and freed His chosen, His saints, His brethren and children from servitude and the penalty of the Law, from the judgment of sin, and from the fearful terrors of the threatened death in such a manner that their human weakness and mistakes will, for His sake, be no more counted against them as sin, if they will but walk before Him with penitent believing hearts, and will steadily cling to His Word with firm and sure consciences" (p. 827).

"(Christ) knew no sin . . . but Paul calls Him sin [2 Corinthians 5:21] in the Hebrew idiom, that is, a sacrifice for sin. . . . (p. 144; cf. p. 429).

"Behold, worthy reader, all those who sincerely believe in this glorious love of God, this abundant, great blessing of grace in Christ Jesus, manifested toward us, are progressively renewed through such faith; their hearts are flooded with joy and peace; they break forth with joyful hearts in all manner of thanksgiving; they praise and glorify God with all their hearts . . . " (p. 144; cf. p. 885).

"Tell me, beloved . . . what does it avail to go by the mere name of a Christian brother if we have not the inward, evangelical faith, love, and irreproachable life of the true brother of Jesus Christ?" (p. 413).

"Truth will remain truth forever. If you are not converted to a better and a Christian mind . . . if you do not repent and become like innocent, simple children, you cannot enter the kingdom of heaven" (p. 208; cf. p. 90).

"That which is born of flesh and blood . . . is carnally minded . . . altogether deaf, blind, and ignorant in divine things" (pp. 54-55).

"In a word, the birth of earth makes earthly minded, and the birth of heaven makes heavenly minded" (p. 416).

"The words of Paul shall never be broken, If any man have not the Spirit of Christ, he is none of his. Romans 8:9. And, where the Spirit is there shall also be the fruits of the Spirit . . ." (p. 448).

"Scripture teaches openly that there is no Christian save he who is in Christ and has His Spirit . . ." (p. 645).

". . . The merciful and great God has, in these last days of unrighteousness, once more allowed the noble and worthy Word of His divine grace to be known again to some in pure, Christian understanding, and since He has placed it as a pure light in the midst of darkness, the means whereby He in everlasting love will assemble unto Himself for the great and dark day an obedient and willing church through the revelation of His holy Word and the enlightenment of His eternal Spirit, and since He has chosen them as His own peculiar people . . . all the gates of hell bestir themselves and rave . . ." (p. 626).

"[The Holy Spirit] is a dispenser of the gifts of God, and that (take note) according to His own will. . . . He guides us into all truth; He justifies us. He cleanses, sanctifies, reconciles, comforts, reproves, cheers, and assures us. He testifies with our spirit that we are the children of God. This Spirit all they receive who believe on Christ . . ." (p. 496).

". . . The foundation on which the entire edifice of our faith must be placed, is Christ Jesus alone. All who are built upon this ground will not be consumed by the fire of tribulation, for they are living stones in the temple of the Lord. They are like gold, silver, and precious stones and can never be made to collapse by such gates of hell as false doctrine, flesh, blood, the world, sin, the devil, water, fire, sword, or by any other means, no matter how sorely they are tried. For they are founded on Christ, confirmed in the faith, and assured in the Word through the Holy Ghost that they cannot be deflected from the pure and wholesome doctrine of Christ by all the furious and bloody Neros under heaven, with all their cruel tyranny. They are not to be diverted from an unblamable and pious life which is of God, as we have seen in many places for more than twenty years past, for they are as immovable as Mount Zion, like firm pillars, brave knights and pious, valiant witnesses of Christ. They have fought unto death, and do so daily (God be praised eternally). I speak of those who have the Spirit and Word of the Lord" (pp. 329-330).

". . . Arouse yourselves, repent; believe Christ; seek, fear, and love God with all your hearts; then the Word of the Lord and His unction will teach you . . . the Lord . . . desires obedience and not sacrifice. He desires the whole heart, the entire man. With Him neither church nor alms matter ultimately; neither words nor deeds, as long as you do not manifest a new heart and life . . . " (pp. 140-141).

"[True] Christians obey His Word, walk in His commandments, bow to His scepter, and quiet their consciences with His grace, atonement, merit, sacrifice, promise, death, and blood. They believe and confess that if they forsake His Word and will, willfully transgress His commandments, and live after the flesh, that God will require it at their hands and punish them eternally with the fire of His wrath, through His righteous judgment. For if those who willfully transgressed the law of Moses had to die without mercy upon the testimony of two or three witnesses (Hebrews 10:28) how much more will they be punished who trample underfoot the Son of God, who esteem the pure blood of the New Testament as impure, and profane the Holy Spirit of grace? (p. 392).

Chapter 8: *God and Israel*

On Israel's rejection of Jesus the Christ:

"Oh, that Israel had acknowledged the most glorious promise of grace which was given them and their fathers in regard to the promise of the seed, land, kingdom, and glory! And that they had considered the blessings of God so abundantly shown to them and their fathers when He miraculously led them from the land of Egypt and let them pass through the Red Sea (Exodus 14:22): when He went before them by day in a pillar of cloud and led the way; and by night in a pillar of fire (Exodus 13:21); when He gave them bread from heaven (Exodus 16:4); when He gave them to drink from the rock (Exodus 17:6); when their clothes nor their shoes waxed old (Deuteronomy 29:5); when He scattered the giants from before them; when He led them into the promised land flowing with oil, milk, and honey; when He gave them fortified cities and well-built houses full of gold and silver, which they had not built; and vineyards which they had not planted (Deuteronomy 6:11); when He gave them these not for their righteousness' sake but out of grace, and because He would fulfill His promise which He had sworn to Abraham, Isaac, and Jacob. Yes, He gave it as a permanent possession if they should abide in His holy Word, and walk in His divine commandments, statutes, and righteousness, as Moses the faithful servant had repeatedly taught and commanded them. Besides, He gave them grain, oil, wine, peace, freedom, religion, and a fame above all the peoples round about; for there was no people under the heavens which was like unto them. Deuteronomy 4. He led them by the hand as a young child; carried them in His blessed arms; and girded Himself about them as a girdle, as Jeremiah has it, raising up among them His righteous men and prophets who spoke unto them the words of the Lord, kindly reproving all disobedient transgressors and gently comforting the pious hearts with the gracious promise of life both temporal and eternal.

"Oh, that the children of Israel had sincerely acknowledged all these and many other favors. Then they never would have departed so shamefully from the Word, law, will, and commandments of God their Savior and Deliverer, who dealt with them in such a fatherly way. But because they did not acknowledge the gracious benefits which the Lord showed to them, and because they did not fear the righteous judgments against them, therefore the wicked, blind flesh and the adulterous spirit of idolatry so misled them, and so estranged them from God, and made them so drunk and mad that they acted worse than the Gentiles which were before them, whom God had on account of their sinfulness rejected and scattered, as the holy prophets in many Scriptures proclaim.

"Oh, dreadful wrath of God! It cannot fail: If we reject grace, light, truth, righteousness, salvation, true religion, life, heaven, and the benediction, and God Himself, we must by His righteous judgment, without fail, fall heir to wrath, darkness, falsehood, unrighteousness, and idolatry, and at the end eternal damnation, death, hell, the curse, and the devil himself.

". . . I find in all the Scriptures how severely God has always from the beginning of the creation punished all transgression of His divine Word and all disobedience . . . " (pp. 297-298).

"Moreover, the Lord says concerning His servant David: My mercy will I keep for him forevermore, and my covenant shall stand fast with him. His seed also will I make to endure forever, and his throne as the days of heaven. . . . It reads further: if his children forsake my law. Now it is plain that this should not be understood of the physical children of the figurative David, for they turned to idolatry and forsook the law of God. For this they were often punished and at last cut from the olive tree as unfruitful branches" (p. 41).

"The prophet Hosea says: For the children of Israel shall abide many days without a king . . . afterward shall the children of Israel return and seek the Lord their God, and David their king, and shall fear the Lord, and His goodness in the latter days. . . .

"The Jews despised this King Christ and therefore they were blinded. Yet they shall return and come to Christ, their King David, as Paul testifies, saying: Blindness in part is happened to Israel, until the fullness of the Gentiles be come in. And so all Israel shall be saved, as it is written: There shall come out of Zion the deliverer, and shall turn away the ungodliness from Jacob. For this is my covenant with them, when I shall take away their sins. Isaiah 59:20. Since Israel is yet to be converted unto Christ, it follows incontrovertibly that the King David, whom the Lord shall seek, can be none other than Christ" (p. 38).

Chapter 9: *The Transformed Disciple*

On the relationship of the Christian to the world, including the state:

"We are to crucify the flesh with its affections and lusts, not to conform to this world, to put off the works of darkness and put on the armor of light; not to love the world, neither the things that are in the world" (p. 113).

"All their thoughts (Christians') are chaste, gentle, peaceful, heavenly, and of the Holy Spirit; all their words are wisdom, truth, doctrine (teaching), admonition in grace, well-seasoned, the words of God spoken at the right time" (p. 411).

"Learn to know what a true Christian is, of whom he is born, how he is minded, what his true intention and ambition [are], and you will find that they are not rebels, murderers, and robbers, as the learned ones [state church leaders] rave, but they are a God-fearing, pious, peaceable people as the Scriptures teach" (p. 556).

"All those who are born of God, who are gifted with the Spirit of the Lord, who are, according to the Scriptures, called into one body and love in Christ Jesus, are prepared by such love to serve their neighbors, not only with money and goods, but also after the example of their Lord and Head, Jesus Christ, in an evangelical manner, with life and blood. They show mercy and love, as much as they can. No one among them is allowed to beg. They take to heart the need of the saints. They entertain those in distress. They take the stranger into their houses. They comfort the afflicted; assist the needy; clothe the naked; feed the hungry; do not turn their face from the poor; do not despise their own flesh" (p. 558).

"... Paul clearly testifies, saying: The fruit of the Spirit is love, joy, peace, longsuffering, gentleness, goodness, faith, meekness, temperance. Not a word is said about taking up the carnal sword or repaying evil for evil. But rather ... recompense to no man evil for evil.... If it be possible, as much as lieth in you, live peaceably with all men. Dearly beloved, avenge not yourselves; but rather give place to wrath: for it is written: Vengeance is mine; I will repay, saith the Lord. Therefore if thine enemy hunger, feed him; if he thrist, give him drink; for in so doing thou shalt heap coals of fire on his head. Be not overcome of evil, but overcome evil with good. How can Christians fight with implements of war? Paul plainly said, Let this mind be in you which was also in Christ Jesus. Now Christ Jesus was minded to suffer; and in the same way all Christians must be minded" (p. 45).

"Seeing then that Christ Jesus is the Prince and the Lord of eternal peace, and since His entire doctrine and life, as also His death has represented, portrayed, and implied naught but peace, as was said, therefore none can be the recipient of His honor and good will, or be given a place in His kingdom save those who have the holy peace of God in their hearts. For His kingdom is the kingdom of peace; it knows no strife, even as it is written in the prophets that in the kingdom of Christ and in His church they beat their swords into ploughshares and sit under their own fig tree and vine, and no more raise up their hands unto warfare. Isaiah 2; Micah 2" (p. 1031).

"If Christ fights His enemies with the sword of His mouth, if He smites the earth with the rod of His mouth, and slays the wicked with the breath of His lips; and if we are to be conformed unto His image, how can we, then, oppose our enemies with any other sword? Does not the apostle Peter say: For even hereunto were ye called, because Christ also suffered for us, leaving us an example, that ye should follow His steps, who did no sin, neither was guile found in His mouth: who, when He was reviled, reviled not again; when he suffered He threatened not; but committed Himself to Him that judgeth righteously? This agrees with the words of John who says, He that abides in Christ walks as Christ walked. Christ Himself says, Whosoever will come after me, let him deny himself, and take up his cross, and follow me. Again, My sheep hear my voice and they follow me.... Ye have heard that it hath been said, An eye for an eye, and a tooth for a tooth: but I say unto you, that ye resist not [him that is] evil: But whosoever shall smite thee on thy right cheek, turn to him the other also" (p. 44).

"Peter was commanded to sheathe his sword. All Christians are commanded to love their enemies; to do good unto those who abuse and persecute them; to give the mantle when the cloak is taken, the other cheek when one is struck. Tell me, How can a Christian defend scripturally retaliation, rebellion, war, striking, slaying, torturing, stealing, robbing and plundering and burning cities, and conquering countries?" (p. 555).

"We publicly and unequivocally confess that the office of a magistrate is ordained of God.... And ... we have obeyed them when not contrary to the Word of God. We intend to do so all our lives.... Taxes and tolls we pay as Christ has taught and Himself practiced. We pray for the imperial majesty, kings, lords, princes, and all in authority. We honor and obey them. 1 Timothy 2:2; Romans 13:1" (p. 549).

"... The civil sword we leave to those to whom it is committed" (p. 200).

"We resist neither the emperor, the king, nor any authority in that to which they are called of God; but we are ready to obey to the death in all things which are not contrary to God and His Word" (p. 118).

Chapter 10: *The Considerate Church Member*

On strife and the need for discipline in the church:

"... He commanded to baptize those who should hear and believe His holy Gospel. Matthew 28:19; Mark 16:16. ...

"Dear reader, it is true that by this commandment the holy church is extended to the Gentiles, to the fulfillment of the prophetic Scriptures which long before had seen this through the Spirit, as Paul proves. Romans 15" (p. 238).

"Remember also how sincerely the holy Paul admonished the Philippians that they should guard against strife, evildoers, and the concision. He taught the true servants of God that they should shun those who merely failed, it seems, by holding fast to the circumcision which they had received from their fathers and would not admit that it would be abolished in Christ" (p. 169).

"Wherefore, brethren, understand correctly, no one is excommunicated or expelled by us from the communion of the brethren but those who have already separated and expelled themselves from Christ's communion either by false doctrine or by improper conduct.

For we do not want to expel any, but rather to receive; not to amputate, but rather to heal; not to discard, but rather to win back; not to grieve, but rather to comfort; not to condemn, but rather to save. For this is the true nature of a Christian brother" (p. 413).

". . . All those who lead a shameful carnal life, and those who are corrupted by heretical, unclean doctrine (Titus 3:10), and who will not be overcome by the wine and oil of the Holy Spirit, but after they have been admonished and sought in all love and reasonableness remain obdurate . . . should at last in the name of the Lord Jesus by the power of the Holy Spirit, that is, by the binding Word of God, be reluctantly but unanimously separated from the church of Christ, and should therefore . . . be shunned until they repent" (p. 483).

Kitchener-Waterloo Record

J. C. Wenger is a teacher of Historical Theology in the Goshen Biblical Seminary, a member school of the Associated Mennonite Biblical Seminaries, Elkhart, Indiana. Born at Honey Brook, Pennsylvania, December 25, 1910, he is a son of the Lancaster Conference, but he moved with his parents to Bucks County, Pa., as a boy, and was later baptized in the Rockhill congregation of the Franconia Conference.

He studied at Eastern Mennonite and Goshen colleges, and holds degrees from both American and European universities. He was installed successively as a deacon, a minister, and an overseer in the Mennonite Church, and has served on the executive committees of both the district and general conferences, as well as on the Presidium of the Mennonite World Conference. He has also been a member of the executive committee of the Mennonite Historical Society and of the Institute of Mennonite Studies. He has taught at Union Biblical Seminary in India, and at Eastern Mennonite Seminary in Virginia. He has also served on the editorial boards of the *Mennonite Quarterly Review* and of the book series, *Studies in Anabaptist and Mennonite History,* as well as *The Mennonite Encyclopedia.*

He has served the Mennonite Church on its Board of Education and its Publication Board, as well as its Historical Committee, in addition to direct pastoral responsibility.

He is a member of the Committee on Bible Translation which prepared the *New International Version* of the Bible. This is his second commentary on a biblical book.

His wife is the former Ruth D. Detweiler, RN, of Bucks County, Pennsylvania, and they are the parents of two sons and two daughters.

Among his books are *Introduction to Theology, Separated unto God, God's Word Written, The Mennonite Church in America,* and a number of monographs on Anabaptist-Mennonite history and doctrine. He is deeply concerned to see the church seek renewal and greater faithfulness to Christ and his Word.